D1384167

NATURE'S
WAYS

*To my mother, who introduced
me to the natural world.*

NATURE'S WAYS

lore, legend, fact and fiction

RUTH BINNEY

David and Charles

A DAVID & CHARLES BOOK
Copyright © David & Charles Limited 2006

David & Charles is an F+W Publications Inc. company
4700 East Galbraith Road
Cincinnati, OH 45236

First published in the UK in 2006

Text copyright © Ruth Binney 2006

Ruth Binney has asserted her right to be identified as
author of this work in accordance with the Copyright,
Designs and Patents Act, 1988.

A catalogue record for this book is available from
the British Library.

ISBN-13: 978-0-7153-2417-2 hardback
ISBN-10: 0-7153-2417-9 hardback

Printed in Great Britain by CPI Bath Press
for David & Charles
Brunel House   Newton Abbot   Devon

Commissioning Editor Neil Baber
Assistant Editor Louise Clark
Project Editor Beverley Jollands
Designer Emma Sandquest
Production Controller Kelly Smith

Visit our website at www.davidandcharles.co.uk

David & Charles books are available from all good
bookshops; alternatively you can contact our Orderline
on 0870 9908222 or write to us at FREEPOST EX2
110, D&C Direct, Newton Abbot, TQ12 4ZZ (no stamp
required UK only); US customers call 800-289-0963
and Canadian customers call 800-840-5220.

CONTENTS

INTRODUCTION

For as long as I can remember, I have been intrigued by 'nature's ways'. From early in childhood I would walk with my mother along the Grand Western Canal near Tiverton, in Devon, collecting leaves, picking wildflowers (in those days an altogether acceptable activity) and then taking them home to be pressed, identified and named.

There were magical moments – seeing a dragonfly emerge or an adder basking in early spring sunshine – and there was frogspawn to collect in a jar in the hope of nurturing at least a few adult amphibians. Away from the water, up the lane, was the 'wishing tree', and I never missed the ritual of running round it three times and making a secret wish. On holiday in Scotland, I swam in the deep, dark waters of Loch Ness, trying to imagine whether I really was sharing space with the famous monster.

In adulthood I am now more fascinated than ever by plants and animals, not just for themselves, but by the ways that we relate to them and the ways in which they affect our lives. I know for certain that I am not the only person who watches the oaks and ashes in spring to see which is first in leaf (and so predict whether the summer will be wet or dry) and feels a surge of joy at the sight of the first swallow or a kingfisher at any time of year. What strikes me most strongly is that even those of us lucky enough to live in the country are not, as a rule, as close to the plants and animals who share our planet as our forebears were, and that so many of the legends and folktales, myths and superstitions about living things reflect both this past closeness and a desire to explain nature's wonders and mysteries.

When I started to think about this book, and to organize the huge amount of research I had collected, I was overwhelmed by how much there was. However, the main themes that emerged key strongly into the ways in which we relate to plants and animals and tell tales about their origins and behaviour. It quickly becomes clear how we use them as symbols and tokens, how we explain their actions, how they may help, heal and feed us, how they have become the focus of superstitions and sayings and why we should treat them with respect or even fear them. As well as the realities of nature, I also delved into the fascinating world of 'invented' creatures, which reveal yet more secrets of our longstanding relationship with animals and plants.

Once again, I am indebted to my friends and family for their support, especially my husband Donald for his patience while I trawl the shelves of second-hand bookshops and market stalls for tempting volumes, and to my daughter Laura for her constant encouragement. My good neighbours Gordon and Maureen Shaw have provided many valuable snippets from their 'attic collection', notably a source of Romany recipes (which must not, like the others in this book, be tried at home under any circumstances). The London Library, as ever, has proved a treasure trove of books. My thanks go also to my editor Neil Baber and the team at David & Charles, and to Beverley Jollands for her meticulous editing.

More than ever, the plant and animal inhabitants of the natural world deserve our care and respect. By understanding more about the many ways in which they touch our lives – even if these are fanciful – I hope, like me, you will find your love of nature hugely enhanced.

Ruth Binney

ANIMAL WAYS

The characters of animals have become an integral part of our descriptive language. Owls are wise and lions are brave; bears are strong and monkeys mischievous. As they were establishing the first civilizations, humans must have quickly come to recognize which of the creatures who shared their world were harmful and dangerous and which were useful – whether to guard their homes, as means of transport, or as sources of food.

So strongly embedded are the supposed characters of many animals that the ancients believed these creatures to be the embodiments of deities or to be closely linked with them. In countless tales told down the ages – and, of course, in the Bible – the powers of animals are colourfully recounted, often with some kind of moral attached. As a result it has become only natural to think of snakes as evil (though they can also be good), of rats as dirty and of donkeys as stupid. From their typical behaviour, and their place in lore and legend, certain animals have also become symbolic of all kinds of attributes. So the dove is a bird of peace, the eagle an emblem of victory and the swan the symbol of pure beauty.

In folklore, animals can do almost anything. They can be friends and foes to the people with whom they share the planet, and can talk to each other with ease. They can be evil witches and devils in disguise and the objects of hate and opprobrium. They can bring good luck and bad. In real life they can, as our domestic pets, be our dearest companions, to the point of sheer worship, even helping to heal our ills.

LITTLE BIRDS THAT KNOW

Since ancient times birds, because of their keen eyesight and aerial view of the world, have been linked with wisdom and knowledge. Owls and ibises are believed to be especially wise.

A wise old owl sat in an oak,
The more he saw the less he spoke,
The less he spoke the more he heard,
Wasn't that owl a wise old bird?

Thus runs the children's rhyme (which is as much a lesson in listening as on the good sense of the owl, and has the alternative last line 'Why can't we all be like that wise old bird?'). However the owl's association with knowledge stems largely from the fact that the bird was companion to Athene, Greek goddess of wisdom, sciences and arts. So strong was the connection that Athenian coins bearing the head of the goddess on one side were marked on the other with an owl and an olive branch (symbol of peace and plenty) from the tree believed to have been given to the earth by Athene. However, there is no known link between the owl's symbolic wisdom and its naturally 'bespectacled' knowing looks.

In ancient Egypt the god Thoth, creator and commander of the universe, god of writing and knowledge, protector of scribes and keeper of the records of the dead, was commonly depicted with

In the days of King Arthur and his Knights of the Round Table, the owl was linked with the wizard Merlin, and was customarily depicted on his shoulder. The 'real' Merlin was probably a Celtic bard.

In the Christian tradition, the owl is associated with St Jerome, who was described as the fountain of wisdom, a reputation earned from the fact that he was a translator of the Bible and the foremost biblical scholar of his day.

the body of a man and the head of an ibis, whose reputation for wisdom may have stemmed from its annual arrival in Egypt at the time of the Nile's inundation. Later, Thoth became linked with keepers of dangerous secrets and the occult.

THE CRUEL CROCODILE

The crocodile is the embodiment of hypocrisy – the creature who 'smiles' at you, then gobbles you up. The alligator (early writing made no distinction between the two) is equally feared.

The crocodile, described by a 16th-century explorer as 'cowardly on land, cruel in the water', was said to lure its prey with moaning sounds then, having devoured its meal, shed tears of false remorse. Its hypocritical habits are wonderfully evoked by Edmund Spenser in *The Faerie Queene*, in these lines depicting the meeting of 'a weary traveller' and his attacker,

> *Which, in false griefe hyding his harmfull guile,*
> *Doth weep full sore, and sheddeth tender teares:*
> *The foolish man, that pitties all this while*
> *His mournfull plight, is swallowed up unwares...*

It is a widespread urban legend that alligators inhabit the sewers of New York. They are said to be adult versions of small, rejected pets bought in Florida and flushed down toilets.

Outwitting the crocodile: *It takes the cunning of a fox to foil a crocodile, as in this South African folktale. A big crocodile was killing sheep, cattle and people, and the king called a meeting to see how it might be banished. Fox jumped up and said: 'O King, I am small but wisdom surpasses bravery. Why do you wait for your enemy to grow strong? What do I do? I eat crocodiles while they are still in the eggs. Get rid of your enemy before he is stronger than you.'*

Crocodiles do certainly make mournful noises, though their 'tears' are thought by zoologists to be the creature's natural mechanism for shedding excess salt rather than revealing their temperament. And not all who approach are attacked. After feeding, the Nile crocodile will lie with its huge mouth agape and allow small plovers or 'crocodile birds' to clean its mouth, teeth and throat.

Ravens were long feared as harbingers of death. In The Jew of Malta *Marlowe refers to 'The sad presaging raven, that tolls/The sick man's passport in her hollow beak.'*

AVIAN THIEVES

Birds in the crow family, especially magpies, crows, ravens, jays and jackdaws, have a deserved reputation as nature's thieves – and one is the subject of a well-loved opera.

Shiny objects, including money and jewellery, are attractive to these birds, and have led to many stories, including the true one on which Rossini's opera *The Thieving Magpie* is based. In it, a servant girl is executed for stealing from her master but, after her death, it is discovered that the magpie was in fact to blame.

Another story is told by Jonathan Swift in *Thoughts on Various Subjects* of 1711: 'An old miser kept a tame jackdaw, that used to steal pieces of money, and hide them in a hole, which the cat observing, asked why he would hoard up those round shining things that he could make no use of? "Why," said the jackdaw, "my master has a whole chest full, and makes no more use of them than I."'

The corvines are relentless stealers of other birds' eggs and chicks. They nest in colonies of 20 or more birds, using church towers, mills, and the like – any building with a cavity that gives shelter and shade – from where they will sally forth on foraging expeditions.

CUNNING AS THE FOX

Everything about the fox's looks and behaviour portray an expert in cunning. This inveterate night hunter will trick its pursuers by tracking in circles and even by making friends with the dogs trained to chase it down.

Farmer and fox have long had an uneasy relationship. As plunderer of poultry the fox is a hated enemy, but he also catches the rabbits and other vermin that destroy crops. Its nature is contradictory – it is both destructive and creative, bold but timid, defensive yet at ease in almost any environment, from open fields to city streets.

Legends of many lands relate that the vixen is a sorceress in disguise, lurking in the forests and sometimes assuming the looks of a beautiful woman who, once she had cast her evil spell, changed to animal form.

The fox figures widely in fables. In Aesop's story 'The Fox and the Crane' the two creatures are apparently on good terms. Fox invites the bird to share a meal, but for a joke serves soup in flat dishes. Fox laps it up with ease but Crane cannot eat. Crane then invites Fox to dine and serves soup in long-necked bottles, which only Crane, with his long bill, can reach. The moral of the tale is that turning the tables is fair play.

FOXY SAYINGS

The cunning of the fox is cemented into the English language in dozens of sayings, including:

- *When the fox preaches, then beware your geese.*
- *It is an ill sign for a fox to lick a lamb.*
- *The fox preys farthest from his home.*
- *An old fox is not easily snared.*
- *If you deal with a fox, think of his tricks.*

TRICKSTER WAYS OF WOLF AND COYOTE

Many animal characters take on the role of tricksters, able to behave and talk like humans. With the coyote and the wolf such stories undoubtedly arise from observations of the natural cunning that helps these creatures survive in the wild.

No doubt the character and behaviour of the real animals led to their characterization as tricksters. Typical is the contradictory ferocity and skulking cowardice of wolves, including the prairie wolf or coyote. Among Native Americans, stories about this creature abound, with the trickster always on the lookout for opportunities to get his way. Typical is the story of 'Coyote and the Dancing Ducks':

The 'wolf in sheep's clothing' is the trickster in disguise. To 'cry wolf' is to set up a false alarm, like the shepherd boy who cried 'Wolf!' to taunt his neighbours then (with them) was eaten up when the animal really came calling, because no one any longer believed his repeated warnings.

One day, Coyote saw a flock of ducks by a lake. How he fancied a nice duck dinner! He stuffed a bag full of grass and walked past the ducks, singing a catchy tune. 'What's in the bag?' asked a duck. 'Songs,' replied Coyote. 'Please sing your songs for us,' implored the ducks. After much pleading, Coyote agreed, but only if the ducks stood in three lines with the fattest at the front, then closed their eyes and danced and sang as loudly as they could. So Coyote moved up and down the line, thumping the ducks on the head and stuffing the stunned birds into his bag. But one scrawny duck at the back opened his eyes, saw what was going on, and shouted a warning. At this, the surviving ducks made their getaway. Coyote was happy – he had plenty to eat. The ducks went home and mourned their dead, and gave thanks to the Great Duck that one of them had been wise enough to open his eyes, and that the rest had been wise enough to listen to the one who had raised the alarm.

PRICKLY ANIMAL TRICKS

It was once believed that the porcupine could transfix its enemies by shooting its spines at them. Though this is fanciful, the creature retains its place in folklore as an animal never to be underestimated. The hedgehog is another animal that it is prudent to approach with caution.

If you grow fruit, beware – at night, a hedgehog will carry off both apples and grapes on its prickles. And farmers accuse hedgehogs of milking cows during the hours of darkness.

The porcupine's reputation for 'killer quills' probably comes from the fact that if one of its spines becomes embedded in an enemy it is easily shed by the porcupine but, being barbed, is difficult, if not impossible to remove. A porcupine in full attack raises its spines and rattles them together, stamping its feet. The charge is not made head on: instead the creature reverses at speed, ramming its quills into its victim.

As a character in Native American tales, Porcupine regularly encounters other masters of subterfuge, including Coyote. One popular Plains Indian story relates how Porcupine, wanting a meal and also needing to cross a stream, hitches a ride with a buffalo. He is cunning enough to wait until he has been helped across before killing his carrier, but he is out-witted by Coyote. The two have a contest to see who will get the meat, agreeing,

Shakespeare called the hedgehog the 'hedge-pig' because of the snorting sounds it makes. These, in folklore, are warnings that ghouls and ghosts are on the prowl.

at Coyote's suggestion, that whoever manages to jump over the carcass shall have it. Coyote, of course, jumps over but short-legged Porcupine cannot. In revenge Porcupine kills Coyote's children.

SPIDER TALENTS

The 19th-century poem by Mary Howitt that begins '"Will you walk into my parlour?" said the spider to the fly' sums up the spider's cunning in luring its prey into its web. These creatures, feared by many to the point of phobia, get their name from the Old English word *spithra*, a spinner.

'Eight legs, two fangs and an attitude' was the tagline of the 1990 movie Arachnophobia, in which a South American killer spider hitches a lift to the US in a coffin and starts to breed and kill.

In West Africa, where it's said, 'The wisdom of the spider is greater than that of all the world put together', the supreme trickster is the spider Anansi. People also say: 'Woe to him who would put his trust in Anansi – a sly, selfish and greedy fellow.' One story relates how a farmer put a gum doll (a kind of sticky scarecrow) in a field to stop his crops being stolen. Confronted with the doll, Anansi kicked him, but his feet and hands got stuck. Finding his thief, the farmer beat Anansi until his body was flat, and had the mark of the cross on his back.

The arachnids, the zoological group to which spiders belong, are named from the spider's association with Arachne, a Greek girl who was renowned for her skill at spinning and weaving. When she dared to challenge the goddess Athene to a weaving contest, the tactless Arachne completed a wonderful depiction of the loves of the gods. Consumed with fury at her rival's skill, Athene changed Arachne into a spider, condemning her to a life of eternal weaving.

THE MIGHTY WHALE

In lore and legend the whale is renowned more for its symbolic association with rebirth than for its sheer size. And the ancient practice of whaling is surrounded by ritual.

The 'whalebone' used in women's corsetry for nipping in the waist from the early 17th century was not bone at all, but horny baleen. This hangs like combs along the sides of the whale's mouth, and the creature uses it to filter vast quantities of krill and other plankton from the sea.

Whether or not the big fish that swallowed the prophet Jonah in the Bible story was a whale, the two remain inextricably linked. Though ordered by God to travel to Nineveh to reprimand its people for their wickedness, Jonah instead boarded a boat sailing across the Mediterranean. When the ship hit a storm Jonah confessed that this might be God's revenge on him for his disobedience, and was tossed into the sea by the sailors – where he was swallowed by a 'fish'. Despite his pleas to the Almighty, Jonah was kept captive in the animal's stomach for three days. Once free, Jonah completed his mission to Nineveh, where God forgave the people and saved them from destruction.

In medieval allegory Jonah's ordeal became symbolic of the three days which passed between Christ's death and resurrection, when he was believed to be in a dark place 'under the earth'.

WHALING TRADITIONS
Though whaling is now banned in many parts of the world, customs like these reflect past practice:

- *Before a whaling expedition, sprinkling ashes on the ice will dispel evil spirits and protect the whalers.*
- *To celebrate a catch, a whaler's wife and children should dance within a circle made from the bones of a whale.*

- *After a whale has been killed there must be three days of mourning, ending with a ritual return to the sea of any remaining flesh, so that both the spirit and the body of the animal may be reborn.*

THE PELICAN OF CHARITY

In Christian symbolism the pelican is the bird of charity, a tradition that has arisen from a misinterpretation of both the creature and its behaviour. In some old bestiaries, the pelican was virtually interchangeable with the phoenix.

According to ancient lore the pelican pecks at its breast and makes itself bleed; it is this blood on which the chicks feed. A more embroidered tale relates that the female pelican, provoked to anger by her growing young, kills them. But three days later the father returns to the nest, covers the dead chicks with his wings, smites himself in the chest and pours his blood over them to bring them back to life.

It is the birds' sacrifice of body and blood – which is

comparable to Christ's sacrifice in giving his life to save others – that lies behind pelican symbolism. The scene of the pelican feeding blood to her chicks was adopted as a heraldic device by medieval knights. It became known as 'The Pelican in Her Piety' and can still be seen in coats of arms and in the stained glass windows of churches all over Europe. And in *Hamlet* Shakespeare has the bereaved Laertes declare:

> *To his good friends thus wide I'll ope my arms,*
> *And like the kind life-rendring pelican,*
> *Repast them with my blood.*

It is perhaps confusion with the flamingo, which secretes dark red 'crop milk' into its mouth and ejects it to feed its young, that led to the pelican's reputation. Also, the bird often keeps its bill tucked close to its chest as it feeds its brood.

VIGILANT BIRDS

Whether they watch and wait in silence or noisily announce the approach of danger, the crane, cockerel and goose are all renowned for their vigilance.

The crane, according to Aristotle, holds a stone in its claw to keep itself awake while waiting at the waterside for its prey to come within reach. If the bird drops off to sleep the stone falls with a splash, which wakes it up. This may explain why the crane, with its naturally watchful habits, was adopted in medieval times (when awareness of an enemy's approach was a critical survival skill) as a symbol of vigilance.

It is said that no evil spirit would dare to make an appearance at Christmas time because in this season 'Chanticleer clamours the livelong night'.

The cockerel, by contrast, though it

may wait quietly, announces the end of its watch – whether impending evil or merely the arrival of the dawn – with cacophonous crowing. In Christianity it is associated with vigilance against the Devil's wiles and with the incident before Jesus's arrest and trial when he correctly predicted that, before the cock had crowed three times, Peter would 'deny him thrice'. A cock on a church tower or weathervane waits to call both the faithful and the wavering to come to worship. Linking this with the St Peter story, Spenser, in his poem *The Faerie Queene*, writes:

What time the native Bellman of the
       night,
The bird that warnèd Peter of his fall,
First rings his silver bell t'each sleepy
       wight, [person]
That should their mindes up to
       devotion call.

A COMPLETE TURKEY

The bird that graces our dinner tables at Christmas and Thanksgiving is renowned for its lack of guile in allowing itself to be caught and eaten, as well as for its gobbling voice.

The turkey was widely regarded as an interloper when it arrived in Europe from America in the early 16th century and was said to have 'violated the rights of hospitality'. In a 19th-century drawing that expresses the unworthiness of this sentiment a turkey cock is shown, with plumes spread, meeting a proud cockerel, the spurs on its legs lifted ready to attack. Underneath is a verse from Leviticus: 'And if a stranger sojourn with thee in your land ye shall not vex him.'

In its native lands the turkey is thought by some to be a cowardly creature; and certain tribes refused to eat its meat lest they be similarly afflicted. As for its voice, one Cherokee Indian tale tells how the turkey, regretting its feeble tones, asked the grouse to teach it to call more loudly. The grouse accepted, but asked for payment in return. The turkey offered some feathers (which the grouse is said to wear round its neck to this day), but when the time came for the turkey to try out his improved voice he got so agitated that he could only let out a gobble.

In the turkey trot, an American folk dance, partners flap their arms at each other like turkey wings. 'Turkey in the Straw' is traditionally danced to the accompaniment of fiddles and banjos.

SAFE WITH THE DOLPHINS

The notion that dolphins can rescue people from drowning or guide them safely through the water goes back centuries. Today it is claimed that dolphin therapy may be a cure for mental ills.

On a Mediterranean sea journey in the 7th century BC the Greek poet and harpist Arion was set upon by sailors who discovered that he was carrying gold – his prize for winning a musical competition. Before they threw him overboard, the sailors granted Arion's request to play one final melody. Attracted by the beauty of his music, a school of dolphins swam around the ship. Arion leapt into the sea and was carried to safety on a dolphin's back. Dolphins also attended deities, notably the sea-god Poseidon, whose seashell chariot they pulled through the waters, and it was after Cretan sailors had been guided there by a dolphin sent by Apollo that the famous oracle was founded at Delphi.

If you should die at sea, dolphins may save your corpse from being eaten by the fishes. It is said that dolphins know by the smell of a dead man whether or not he has ever killed and eaten one of their kind. If they judge him not guilty, they will bring his body to shore, intact, for his relatives to find. In Christian legend, the body of Lucian of Antioch, who was martyred in 312 CE, was brought ashore by a dolphin after it had been thrown into the sea to deny the saint a Christian burial.

Saved from oneself: *Therapists have found that swimming with dolphins is an excellent remedy for depression.*

THE PURE AND GENTLE DOVE

Especially when feathered in white – the colour of purity – the dove is the perfect symbol of the unde-filed simplicity of the soul. Its special significance in the Judeo-Christian tradition comes from its many appearances in the Bible.

It is the dove's gentle demeanour and quiet habits that have led to its symbolic association with the best behaviour, but most significantly it represents the Holy Spirit at Christ's baptism. St Luke's Gospel records: 'During a general baptism of the people, when Jesus had been baptized and was praying, heaven opened and the Holy Spirit descended on him in bodily form like a dove, and there came a voice from heaven, "You are my beloved Son; in you I delight".' The symbolic use of the bird on this occasion was no accident, since it had long been associated with the Jewish rite of purification.

The dove was the bird that Noah sent out from the Ark to see if the flood had subsided. When it returned with 'an olive leaf plucked off' in its beak he knew that this was so. Ever since, the dove and olive branch have been symbols not only of peace and gentleness between God and humans but also between nations.

DOVE DEEDS AND LORE

• *Doves get their scientific family name Columbidae from their association with St Columba, who had a vision of the Holy Spirit in the form of a dove.*
• *If you make three wishes on hearing the first dove in spring they will all come true.*
• *The dove lays only two eggs because she has pride in – and concern for – the family she will raise.*
• *The dead may be reincarnated as doves.*

THE TALE OF  THE CAMEL'S HUMP

Though valued for their swiftness and staying power, camels have a lasting reputation for stubbornness. And people 'get the hump' when they are generally dissatisfied with life.

Rudyard Kipling used the camel's shape and its character to wonderful effect in his story of 'How the Camel Got His Hump'. 'In the beginning of years,' it starts, 'when the world was new and all, and the Animals were just beginning to work for Man, there was a Camel, and he lived in the middle of a Howling Desert because he did not want to work; and besides, he was a Howler himself. So he ate sticks and thorns and tamarisks and milkweed and prickles, most 'scrutiating idle; and when anybody spoke to him he said "Humph!" Just "Humph" and no more.'

The Camel goes on saying 'Humph' until 'the Djinn in charge of All Deserts' puts an actual 'humph' on his back which, because he missed three days work, allows him to go three days without eating. But, as Kipling concludes, 'We call it a "hump" now, not to hurt his feelings, and he has never yet learned how to behave.'

Someone who 'strains at a gnat and swallows a camel' is a person who makes a fuss about minor misdemeanours but then commits major offences. In this context the word 'strain' means to strain off (as you would to get rid of an insect in a glass of wine).

Though they may be stubborn, camels are certainly not stupid. The one named Al Kaswa was the favourite of Muhammad, and the mosque at Aqaba marks the spot where the creature knelt when the Prophet fled from Mecca.

THE STUPID ASS

The ass takes centre stage in stories that epitomize stupidity (though it does have redeeming features), but it was once associated with evil. We are all, on occasion, likely to make asses of ourselves.

To the Egyptians, an ass was to be approached with care, and to meet a red ass (one the colour of blood) was believed to be fatal to the soul, preventing it attaining the hereafter. It was associated with Seth, the god of chaos and evil, who murdered his brother, Osiris.

Of the 27 tales that Aesop tells about the ass, typical is 'The Ass Who Was Taken for a Lion': 'An ass, clothed in the skin of a lion, passed himself off in the eyes of everyone as a lion, and made everyone flee from him, both men and animals. But the wind came and blew off the lion's skin, leaving him naked and exposed. Everyone then fell upon him when they saw this, and beat him with sticks and clubs.' The moral is, be ordinary and poor: pretensions will make you an object of ridicule.

THE PROVERBIAL ASS

The creature's character is embedded
in the language of proverbs:
- *Every ass thinks himself worthy to stand with the king's horses. (A distorted idea of equality.)*
- *He is an ass that brays against another ass. (The epitome of foolishness.)*
- *Every ass likes to hear himself bray. (It is foolish to talk and not listen.)*
- *Wherever an ass falls, there will he never fall again. (Even the stupid can learn by experience.)*

HUMBLE DONKEY AND GENTLE LAMB

It is largely from their association with Christianity that the donkey and the lamb have acquired their reputations for goodness, and more specifically for gentleness and humility.

The donkey or ass makes two central appearances in the life of Jesus. After the Nativity, when they had been warned of Herod's evil intent to kill all male children under two years old, Mary and Joseph, with the infant Jesus, fled to Egypt on a donkey. In medieval France their escape was celebrated in the Feast of the Ass, on 14 January. As part of the celebrations, a girl carrying a baby was led through the streets on a donkey, but the Church took measures to stop the festival when, over the years, it degenerated into a burlesque, ending in a ceremony in which both priest and people brayed like asses.

That Jesus is 'the lamb of God, which taketh away the sin of the world' explains Christ's association with this gentle animal, created to be without malice. Jesus was also called 'the Paschal lamb' because this creature, traditionally sacrificed at the Jewish Passover, is linked with St Paul's testament: 'For even Christ our Passover lamb is sacrificed for us.'

THE DEVIL'S GOAT

When, in medieval times, Satan was believed to take on the form of an animal, the goat was most often cast in this evil role. Other vile associations come from the ritual of the scapegoat.

The goat's evil reputation stems from accounts such as that of the trials in 1335 of Anne-Marie de Georgel and Catherine Delort, who were accused of having had sexual relations with the Devil in the form of a goat. And in 1460 the witches of Arras were condemned because they worshipped and made offerings to the Devil in similar guise. The trial record made special mention of the fact that 'with candles in their hands they kiss the hind parts of the goat that is the Devil'.

The concept of the scapegoat, an animal that takes on the sin of another, comes from an ancient Jewish ritual described in Leviticus. Two goats were taken to the altar of the tabernacle, where the high priest cast lots, earmarking one animal for Yaweh (the Lord) the other for Azazel (the evil one). The Lord's goat was sacrificed, while the scapegoat, though spared, was doomed to take on the sins of the people and the priest. After the ceremony it was led away and allowed to escape into the wilderness, carrying the sins with it.

The 13th-century monk Matthew Paris told of a black billy goat, said to have been an evil spirit that carried the body of King William II (William Rufus) to judgment. The king, hated by his subjects for his cruelty, had been shot and killed by an arrow while out hunting in 1100.

THE LOATHSOME PIG

The unfortunate pig is often the butt of opprobrium, the animal having been associated over the centuries with demons. It is one of the 'unclean' animals that Jews are forbidden to eat.

When God advised Noah which animals he was to take into the ark he distinguished between 'clean' and 'unclean' animals. The pig is considered unclean because it has cloven hooves but, unlike a cow, does not chew the cud. Isaiah lists, among many abominations, 'he that offereth an oblation as if he offered swine's blood'.

In the New Testament, pigs were cursed when Jesus drove unclean spirits into the bodies of the 'Gadarene swine' which, turned mad, rushed to their own destruction. Small holes in the creatures' forefeet are believed to be the marks where the Devil's disciples entered them.

Compared with its ancestor the wild boar – which

Like goats, pigs were believed to be the Devil in disguise, especially in the form of the Black Boar. Or they might be the incarnations of witches. In 1457 a pig was even tried and condemned to death, though her piglets were saved. The Yird (earth) Pig was believed to roam graveyards, feasting on the bodies of the dead.

not only grubbed in the undergrowth for nuts and roots but raided rabbit burrows and even, reputedly, killed fawns as they slept – the pig is a benign creature. When chased, said the 19th-century French zoologist J H Fabre, the boar 'sharpens its tusks and works its drivelling jaws. Its mane stands erect on head and back; its little eyes, inflamed with fury, resemble two glowing coals.'

The same author declares, 'Despite all its improvements the [domestic] pig still remains a coarse animal ... addicted to gluttony' and 'devotes itself unreservedly to the gratification of its voracious appetite ... Its gluttony extends even to the devouring of kitchen refuse.' It is lazy, he says, 'always either sleeping, stretched out on its side in the full enjoyment of digestion, or rooting in the ground in the hope of some chance additional titbit, however small.'

THE LOVABLE PORKER
The intelligence of the pig is celebrated, not least for its ability to hunt out edible treasures. Pigs even get some of the best roles on TV and in the movies.

In ancient Crete, the pig was so highly esteemed that it became an object of worship. Pigs – usually small, suckling pigs – were sacrificed to Demeter, goddess of the earth and fertility, and eating the animal's meat, except as a sacrifice, was taboo. The ancient Celts also worshipped the pig, and considered pork the best of all the meats.

St Anthony the Great, one of the early Church's Desert Fathers, was adopted as the patron saint of swineherds because he once tended pigs himself, and wandered the desert with a pig always at his side. Once, so the story goes, when fire existed only in Hell, people were freezing to death and came to St Anthony for help. He went to the inferno but was refused entry, though the pig was allowed in. It ran about creating havoc, until the demons were forced to ask the saint to come in and retrieve it. While doing so, St Anthony collected some fire in his staff and, on his return, he gave it to the world.

In all their truffle hunts, pigs have rarely been as successful as in 1858 when the Marquis des Isnard witnessed the unearthing of a monster haul weighing 55lb (25kg). However, today experts favour dogs over pigs for truffle hunting, because pigs have a tendency to consume the delicacies they unearth.

The smallest pig in a litter is still sometimes called a 'Tantony pig', which comes from the medieval custom of donating the runt of a litter to the monks of St Anthony's hospital in London for the benefit of the inmates.

FICTIONAL FAVOURITES
Pigs that hit the heights:

Miss Piggy – *Muppet superstar.*
Babe – *the pig-turned-sheepdog, who wins the prize.*
Porky the Pig – *the stuttering straight man and Warner Brothers first cartoon star.*
Empress of Blandings – *the prize-winning sow of P.G. Wodehouse's novels.*
Napoleon – *the pig who is the self-appointed leader in George Orwell's* Animal Farm.
Piglet – *from the Disney animated version of* Winnie-the-Pooh.
Wilbur – *the main character in* Charlotte's Web *by E.B. White.*

BEWARE THE BATS

Many features of bats conspire to underline their sinister reputation – not least their leathery wings, fluttering flight and their habit of roosting in caves, ruins and other spooky places.

Bats' blood was regularly used by sorceresses in their black masses and by witches in their flying ointment.

Until its mammalian identity was clarified, the bat was a mystery. Known as a flitter-mouse or *avis, non avis*, meaning 'bird and not bird', in folklore it took a dual role, as both the symbol of the soul and the personification of the evil one who dwells in darkness. As the Devil in disguise, bats were hounded and killed from ancient times. Even in the 20th century they were sometimes nailed with outstretched wings to the doors of Sicilian homes to protect their occupants from disaster.

Bats could also, it was thought, be the embodiment of vampires – the living dead who fed on the blood of their human victims – or witches in animal form, which made it particularly unlucky to find a bat in the house or even flying around it. A bat circling a house three times was taken as a sign of impending death. And seeing bats ascending into the air, then flying straight down again, was said to indicate that witches were due to meet nearby. As an antidote to such danger, it was thought that protection could be gained by carrying a bat bone.

To rid people of evil spirits it is a widespread practice to 'magic' out a bat, usually via the mouth. One story relates how a Frenchman suffering from melancholia was brought a bat in a bag by a surgeon, a physician and a priest. While the surgeon made an incision in the man's side – and the priest prayed – the physician released the bat. The patient, convinced that the force of evil had departed, recovered instantly.

VULTURES: BIRDS OF INFAMY

It is largely their habit of feeding on the bodies of dead creatures – and circling above the ground ever hopeful of a carrion meal – that has earned the vultures their poor reputation. On the plus side, they are believed to have protective powers.

'The repulsive nature of its food,' said the 19th-century author Emma Phipson of the vulture, 'together with its ungainly appearance and great voracity, are some excuse for the disgust it has inspired.' Added to this, its hooked beak, bald head and unattractive feathers make for a bird once dubbed a 'feathered hyena' and, for its ability to kill live animals, 'the enemy of shepherds'.

The vulture's baldness came about, the Iroquois say, because when birds were first searching for feathers they sent the vulture to acquire their new 'clothes'. On his long journey the vulture, lacking food, was forced to eat carrion and, when he reached his desti-

The eggs of other birds are a favourite food of vultures. The Egyptian vulture, presented with the tempting prospect of an ostrich egg, will even (having a bill too small to grasp the egg whole) pick up stones in its beak and hurl them at the egg until the shell breaks.

Usually depicted as a woman, wearing a vulture headdress or with the head of a vulture, the Egyptian goddess Nekhbet was the protector of women in childbirth and of newborn babies.

nation, he greedily chose the best plumage for himself. But his headdress was so weighty that he was forced to remove it, which is why he has been bald ever since.

THE SWAN'S PURE BEAUTY

Once the symbol of the Virgin Mary, the swan is a bird of purity and beauty. Tales abound of swans being transformed into lovely women, and vice versa.

It is said in Ireland that the souls of virtuous maidens dwell in swans. The birds pulled the chariots of Apollo and Venus, and are said to be so sacred that to kill one is to bring death upon the 'murderer' himself. In Greek legend, Zeus transformed himself into a swan to seduce Leda, the mother of Helen of Troy.

The swan has long associations with kings. Edward I adopted it as a heraldic device and at the Feast of the Swan in 1306 his son took an oath on two swans with gilded beaks to avenge a murder committed by Robert the Bruce.

Of the many tales of swan maidens, typical is the one in which a man, having seen a flock of swans alight on the water and watched while they shed their feathers (revealing themselves as beautiful maidens) steals the robes of one of them. He marries her and all goes well until she discovers her feather dress in a cupboard, puts it on and disappears forever.

The purity of the swan and the story of Leda were used by Edmund Spenser in his poem 'Prothalamion', which describes a pair of young brides as two swans:

> *Two fairer Birds I yet did never see;*
> *The snow which doth the top of Pindus strew*
> *Did never whiter shew*
> *Not Jove himselfe, when he a Swan would be,*
> *For love of Leda, whiter did appeare;*

Yet Leda was (they say) as white as he,
Yet not so white as these, nor nothing neare;
So purely white they were.

THE VICTORY EAGLE

The 'king of birds', with super-keen eyesight, soaring flight and powerful beak and talons, the eagle has always been held in the highest esteem and has been adopted as a symbol by rulers and nations down the ages.

As the bird that represents triumph over evil, the eagle was sacred to Zeus. To show its power, which included immunity from lightning strikes, it was depicted holding both a snake and a thunderbolt and was revered as the equal of the sun.

> *A silver eagle was the icon of the Roman Republic, while a golden one symbolized the Roman Empire.*

In the Hindu *Rig-Veda*, the eagle is the bringer to earth of the sacred *soma*, an intoxicating drink of divine power.

An eagle is said to have lifted, and then replaced, the helmet of Tarquinius Priscus, foretelling that he would become king of Rome – a prediction that came true in 616 BC. Roman legions, who used the eagle as their standard (because it was sacred to Jupiter), would set up winter quarters where there was an eagle's eyrie nearby.

EAGLE SYMBOLS

- *The Sioux sport eagle feathers in their war bonnets as a sign of victory.*
- *The American eagle was adopted as a national symbol in 1782.*
- *Poland's red eagle is depicted on a white background on the national flag.*

- *The Emperor Napoleon, who loved all things Roman, copied them by adopting the eagle as his symbol.*
- *The double-headed eagle was adopted as a national symbol by both Germany and Austria.*

BEE MESSENGERS

Whether flying singly or in swarms, bees are widely believed to be messengers of the gods and as such need to be kept happy and informed. As a swarm their behaviour may portend good or evil, depending on the circumstances.

The most universal means of keeping bees happy (so that they will return to their hives and make honey) is to tell them at once of a death in the family. Recommended ways of doing this include tying black crape around the hive and bringing them food such as funeral biscuits soaked in wine or spicy funeral cake. They should also, it is said, be told of good news, as Rudyard Kipling advises in 'The Bee-boy's Song':

A German folktale relates that bees were created so that they could supply wax for church candles. It was a common practice in medieval England for people to leave money in their wills to pay for the beeswax candles to light their funerals.

> *Marriage, birth or buryin'*
> *News across the seas,*
> *All your sad or merryin'*
> *You must tell the bees.*

Bees swarm as they follow a virgin queen out of the hive, at which time they can aggressively sting any human or animal who interferes with their determined journey to found a new colony.

Swarms of bees also make legendary appearances, as in the Irish story of the 6th-century St Gobnait: when her territory was being invaded she routed the enemy by holding up a small hive of bees, which swarmed and stung the invaders in the eyes, so blinding and dispersing them.

Zeus, the father of the Greek gods, was believed to have been born in a cave of bees and fed by them, and he was given the title Melissaios, or 'bee man'. Meliteus, Zeus's son, whose mother was a nymph, was hidden from Hera (Zeus's consort) in a wood and she was also nourished by bees.

THE HELPFUL ROBIN

There are few more endearing birds
than the robin redbreast, which is not
afraid to come close to humans and
their habitations. It is kindly regarded
because of its legendary attention
to the dying Jesus and its role as a
bringer of fire.

*Assisted by the wren,
the robin was said to
have covered the dead,
unburied bodies of the
Babes in the Wood with
moss and leaves.*

When, on Good Friday, a prickle
from the crown of thorns was pressing

*Because it is believed
to carry a drop of God's
blood in its veins, it is
extremely unlucky to
kill a robin. Even an
errant cat, it is said, will
lose a limb if it murders
this bird.*

deep into the Saviour's brow, the robin,
it is said, flew to the Cross and tried to
remove the thorn. As it was doing so, a
drop of Christ's blood fell on to its breast,
staining it forever. Another similar story
ends with the bird injuring itself in its
task, with the same result.

The robin is also renowned as the
bird that brought fire to the world – but
got its breast singed in the attempt. And

according to Welsh legend the robin is red from being
burned as it brought cooling waters to wicked souls
being consumed by the fires of Hell. A verse by the early
19th-century poet John Greenleaf Whittier is based on
this folktale:

> 'Nay,' said the Grandmother, 'have you not heard
> My poor bad boy, of the fiery pit,
> And how drop by drop, this merciful bird
> Carries the water that quenches it?

> 'He brings cool dew in his little bill
> And lets it fall on the souls of sin
> You can see the mark on his red breast still
> Of fires that scorch as he drops it in.'

HIPPO LORE

**Often identified as the Behemoth of the Bible, the
hippopotamus or 'water horse' is a symbol of power
and strength. Recently, it has also become the subject
of an urban myth.**

That the Egyptian word for the hippopotamus was
p-ehe-mau, which became transmuted into the Hebrew
word *b'hemah*, 'beast', is one of the theories behind the
link between this creature and the huge animal that God
described to Job. Behemoth represented the strength and
intelligence that could deliver people from death:

> What strength is in his loins!
> What power in the muscles of his belly!
> His tail is rigid as a cedar, the sinews of his flanks
>   are tightly knit;
> His bones are like tubes of bronze, his limbs like
>   iron bars.

The hippo's habit of living in the water during the day is explained in the Nigerian folktale of the hippo king called Isantim and his seven large, fat wives. Isantim held a feast for the other animals, but challenged them to tell him his name, and when they failed he sent them away hungry. The tortoise asked what he would do if his name was discovered and the hippo said it would bring shame on him and he would leave the land to live in the river. While the hippo and his wives were bathing one day the tortoise overheard one of the wives calling his name. He revealed it at the next feast. The hippo, shamed by the discovery, went down to the water and stayed there, coming ashore only in darkness.

A dwarf named Od, so one of the top urban legends of 2005 relates, was swallowed by a circus hippopotamus in a freak accident in Thailand. One wayward bounce off a trampoline launched the dwarf into the animal's open jaws, which, by reflex, closed instantly.

THE MIGHTY ELEPHANT

The elephant is so strong that even its image, carried as a talisman, is believed to confer similar power on the wearer. The creature's amazing memory, long renowned, is now a proven fact.

In Indian tradition the earth is held in the universe by eight pairs of elephants which, when they grow tired and shake their burden, cause earthquakes to occur. These creatures are named the Lokpalas. Hindus also believe that the warlike god Indra, symbol of prosperity and all-conquering temporal power, rode the earth on the back of an elephant.

In African fables the elephant is the wise chief who impartially settles disputes among the forest creatures. One story is of a hunter who found an elephant skin near Lake Chad and hid it. Soon afterwards he spotted a large but beautiful girl crying because she had lost her 'clothes'. The hunter promised her new clothes and married her, and they had many large children. One day, when the family had run out of grain, the hunter's wife discovered her elephant skin hidden at the bottom of the barn. She put it on and went back to the bush to live as an elephant again. Her human sons became the ancestors of the clan who not only have the elephant as their totem but have nothing to fear from these creatures, who are their kin.

It is true that elephants have truly prodigious memories, especially for the odours of their enemies and members of their family. Each herd follows the routes or 'elephant roads' remembered in detail by the matriarch, the senior female.

> *A 'white elephant' is a euphemism for an unwanted object, especially one that is expensive to maintain. The expression comes from the rare, high-maintenance creatures given by the king of Siam (now Thailand) to those on whom he wished financial disaster.*

DIRTY RATS

These proverbial deserters of sinking ships, rats are generally reviled for their fecundity, destructive habits and their ability to carry disease.

Shakespeare eloquently expresses the link between rats making their escape before a voyage and disaster at sea in *The Tempest*, when Prospero describes to Miranda how:

> *… they hurried us aboard a bark,*
> *Bore us some leagues to sea; where they prepar'd*
> *A rotten carcass of a boat, not rigg'd,*

> *The bad habits of rats which 'fought the dogs and bit the cats,/And bit the babies in the cradles' were the subject of Robert Browning's poem 'The Pied Piper of Hamelin', in which the piper's playing lures both rats and children to their deaths.*

Nor tackle, sail, nor mast; the very rats
Instinctively had quit it.

Rats will gnaw anything, from computer cables to the
traps set out to kill them, but they relish the garbage
of human living. Most seriously, they are notorious as
the vectors (with the help of fleas) of fatal diseases such
as the Black Death of the Middle Ages (see page 127).
Today, rats transmit Weil's disease, listeria, toxoplasmosis
and possibly even SARS, a deadly variant of flu.

RATTY SAYINGS

The rat race – *the struggle to get ahead*
in business, whatever it takes.

'You dirty rat' – *an expression famously*
attributed to the actor James Cagney.
In fact in the 1932 movie Taxi! Cagney
says to actor David Landau: 'Take that,
you dirty yellow rat!'

To rat on someone – *to tell tales about*
them, invariably to their detriment.

King Rat – *the 'leader of the pack'.*

'If you live in a city, you're probably in
close proximity to two rats having sex
right now' – observation of American
rat-watcher Robert Sullivan.

QUIET AS A MOUSE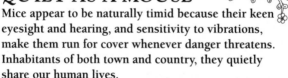

Mice appear to be naturally timid because their keen
eyesight and hearing, and sensitivity to vibrations,
make them run for cover whenever danger threatens.
Inhabitants of both town and country, they quietly
share our human lives.

There are few more engaging descriptions of the
habits of mice than Beatrix Potter's 'Appley Dapply':

Appley Dapply, a little brown mouse,
Goes to the cupboard in somebody's house.
In somebody's cupboard there's everything nice,

Cake, cheese, jam, biscuits – all
charming for mice!
Appley Dapply has little sharp eyes,
And Appley Dapply is so fond
of pies!

Mice are said to embody the soul, which may leave the body during sleep in that form. If such a mouse is killed it is believed to bring about the person's death. Even more ominously, mice are thought to be the inventions of witches, who make them out of pieces of cloth. When a death is imminent, they will leave a house. Mouse colour is important: a black mouse is thought to be stained by sin, while a red one has a pure soul.

A medieval German legend tells of Hatto, Bishop of Mainz, who, when starving people came to him begging for food, instead of helping them locked them in an empty barn where they were killed by fire. A plague of mice followed and the Bishop fled to his 'Mouse Tower' in the middle of the Rhine, but the mice gnawed him to death.

MOUSE TALES

The habits of mice have made them the subjects of many tales – some true, others about endearing fictional inventions such as Mickey Mouse and his fellow cartoon characters.

The silent daring of mice is celebrated by Aesop in his tale 'The Lion Who was Afraid of a Mouse, and the Fox' in which the fox rebukes the lion for fearing the mouse that 'ran all the way up his body' when he was asleep. In reply the lion says: 'It isn't that I was afraid of the mouse, but I was most surprised that there was anyone at all who could be so bold as to run along the body of a sleeping lion.' And the moral? Wise men don't ignore even little things.

To be as poor as a church mouse is to have absolutely nothing. Unlike a home, the church is devoid of tempting edibles.

The zoologist Frank Finn, writing in the early 1900s, says: 'The queer thing is that mice really are very familiar with lions, which seem to consider them beneath their notice … I have seen one run over a lion's foot, and another sit up and trim his whiskers under the terrible paw as it conveniently overhung him where the lion lay.'

IN WORDS AND PICTURES
Mice are widely portrayed – and loved – in fiction, including:

Mickey Mouse – *Walt Disney's most famous character first appeared in* Steamboat Willie *in 1928. His girlfriend Minnie was with him from the start.*

Jerry – *The 'enemy' of Tom the cat; Jerry often gets the upper hand in the cartoons directed by Bill Hanna and Joe Barbera. Tom and Jerry debuted in* Puss Gets the Boot *in 1940.*

The Two Bad Mice – *The subjects of Beatrix Potter's endearingly illustrated story of 1904 narrowly escape discovery after wrecking a doll's house.*

Stuart Little – *The boy who looks like a mouse, and is adopted by a human family but terrorized by cats, came to the essayist EB White in a dream in the 1920s. His story did not appear in print until 1945.*

BEAR STRENGTH
Possessing superhuman strength and with a dangerous propensity for unprovoked attack, the bear is a symbol of power.

The bear is sacred to many of the indigenous North American people, and to the Ainu of Japan it was an important ancestral figure. In Scandinavia the bear was deified as Odin, chief of the gods and deity of wisdom and war. To endow them with bear-like strength, Viking warriors, known as Berserkers, wore

Since the 19th century the bear has frequently been used as a symbol of Russia, especially in the Punch *cartoons of the 1870s drawn by Sir John Tenniel.*

bearskins into battle. The bearskins worn today by Britain's Grenadier Guards were first captured from Napoleon's Imperial Guard at the Battle of Waterloo in 1815.

In the Old Testament, the two boys who shout after the prophet Elisha, 'Go up thou baldhead,' were punished with many others when 'there came forth two she-bears out of the wood and tore forty and two of them'. Before his encounter with Goliath, David killed bears and other wild animals with his sling, which symbolized his spiritual as well as his physical strength.

BAITED AND CELEBRATED BEARS

In Tudor times, every English town of any note had its own bear, and bear baiting was an amusement fit for royalty. In our own times, bears are loved as both toys and fictional characters.

Keeping a town bear afforded symbolic, if not real, protection for its inhabitants. Among the most famous was the bear of Congleton in Cheshire. In 1620 the town needed a new Bible for its chapel but at the same time the town bear died and the money set aside for the Bible was spent instead on a replacement bear.

Dancing bears toured throughout Europe for public amusement, and bear baiting, begun by the Romans, was a popular London amusement by the 12th century, though condemned as 'dishonest' by Edward III. It was also much enjoyed by Elizabeth I. A bear would be chained to a post, able to move but not escape. Dogs would be set on the animal and spectators would bet on whether the dogs or the bear would survive the vicious

fight that ensued. Some of the bears were unfortunate
enough to have long and bloody careers.

BELOVED BEARS

The teddy bear *was named after
President Theodore (Teddy) Roosevelt
by toymakers Morris Michtom and his
wife Rose in the early 1900s, after the
President spared the life of a bear cub.*

Steiff bears, *toys identified by an ear
button, have been made continuously in
Germany since 1905.*

Winnie-the-Pooh, *the honey-loving
invention of AA Milne, is the 'bear with
very little brain' who gets himself into all
kinds of scrapes.*

Rupert Bear, *with his distinctive
yellow and black checked trousers and
scarf and red sweater, first appeared in
a strip cartoon in the* Daily Express *in
1920. The original illustrations were by
Mary Tourtel.*

Yogi Bear, *the animated resident of
Jellystone Park who first appeared in
1958, is a memorable Hanna-Barbera
creation. 'Smarter than the average
bear', his greatest friend is Boo-Boo.*

Paddington Bear, *found by the Brown
family on the eponymous London
station, was a stowaway from 'deepest,
darkest Peru'. Michael Bond's first book
about him was published in 1958.*

THE KING OF BEASTS

**Courage, strength and majesty are the attributes of
the lion, a symbol of Christ and of Britain. The noble
lion, it is said, will not attack a true prince.**

Statues of the king of beasts guarded the entrances
to Egyptian tombs and palaces and sat astride the doors
of Assyrian temples. As a symbol of the sun the lion was
linked with the Egyptian sun god Ra, the life giver.

As the Lion of Judah, Christ was a figure of power
and majesty. In Revelation the writer bemoans the fact
that only 'the Lion from the tribe of Judah, the shoot
growing from David's stock, has won the right to open
the scroll and its seven seals'. This is an expression of the

lion's almighty power. The association between the lion and the Resurrection comes from the fable that the lion cub is born dead but is licked into life by its parents (or awoken by their roaring) in three days.

In Africa, where humans and lions have coexisted for millennia, the lion is revered as a reincarnation of dead ancestors or a spirit that needs to be propitiated. Some African people believe that men can be transformed into lions, thus becoming invulnerable to attacks by other animals. To retain their status, they must leave part of any animals they kill as food for the lions.

The one crucial quality missing in the Lion whom Dorothy meets in The Wizard of Oz *is courage.*

In CS Lewis's stories of Narnia, the land at the back of the wardrobe, the lion Aslan is a metaphor for Christ.

LEONINE MERCY

Though the lion can be roused to anger it also has a reputation for magnanimity – this is another aspect of its nobility and a trait recorded by natural historians down the ages.

The Roman naturalist Pliny described the lion's behaviour like this: 'Only the lion among wild animals shows mercy to suppliants; it spares those bent down before it, and, when angry, turns its rage on men rather than women, and only attacks children when desperately hungry.' Pliny even reported that 'lions understand the meaning of prayers' and wrote that the lion's 'noble spirit is most discernible in dangers: he sneers at

The trademark of Tate and Lyle the British sugar refiners is a dead lion surrounded by bees. It comes from the Biblical story of Samson, who killed a lion and returning later noticed that a swarm of bees had made a honeycomb in the carcass. Samson turned this into a riddle: 'Out of the eater came forth meat and out of the strong came forth sweetness.'

weapons and protects himself for a long time by fearsome threats only …'

In many stories, lions are renowned for their tenderness towards virgins. And in the tale of Androcles and the lion, the Christian Androcles, who once removed a thorn from a lion's paw, is rewarded years later when the same lion refuses to devour him after he has been sentenced to die in a Roman arena.

MENACING BIG CATS

Though the lion and tiger are both large cats, the tiger is never credited with the lion's saving graces. Nor is the leopard, which was once perceived as the embodiment of evil.

Regarding the tiger with respect is only common sense, for of all the big cats it is the one most likely to be a maneater. In Sumatra, it is customary to offer formal apologies to such a creature before it is killed because, like other Asian peoples, Sumatrans believe that having eaten a man a tiger can subsequently make his ghost prowl the jungle and entice other victims to their deaths.

Other means of keeping the tiger happy are never to speak of it disrespectfully and never to trespass on tiger trails. Keeping one's head covered also shows respect. At night, when the tiger's eyes are believed to shine, no sensible person would look back for fear of revealing apprehension to a potential attacker.

Can a man take on the tiger's might? *Various traditional methods are tried, including eating tiger flesh – or, especially, its gall bladder – knotting a tiger whisker into your moustache or beard or carrying a tiger's claw in your pocket. You can also wear a 'tiger's eye' a semiprecious stone (a type of quartz), which glows golden brown. Roman soldiers are said to have worn them to distract their enemies.*

MONKEY BUSINESS

It is their obvious similarities to humans that make monkeys and apes so intriguing and explain their association with mischief. Many of these creatures are thought to have special powers of wisdom.

Playing on their resemblance to humans, a typical Creole folktale tells of Mr Monkey, who falls in love with a beautiful young girl. He dresses as a man and goes to call on her. One day he takes his best friend with him, who hints to the girl's father that there is a secret abroad, but will not reveal it. On Mr Monkey's wedding night the friend (who is jealous of Mr Monkey) sings a song that makes all monkeys dance, whether they wish to or not. Mr Monkey is forced to jump about so wildly that his tail comes out of his clothes, and his true identity is revealed. The father now understands what the secret is, and beats the bridegroom dreadfully, but the friend runs off, dancing and singing.

The Chinese Monkey King, Sun Wu-Kung, is a master shape-shifter and his mischief-making even disrupts the peace of the gods, but he is instrumental in bringing Buddhism from India to China.

In ancient Egypt the baboon was sacred to Thoth, the god of magic and learning. In one myth, Thoth disguises himself as a baboon in order to retrieve Tefnut, daughter of the supreme god Ra, who has fled from her father and is wreaking havoc round the country in the form of a ravening lioness. As a reward for his success Ra appoints Thoth as his representative in the afterlife, judging the souls of the dead.

The Three Wise Monkeys, covering their hands, ears and mouth, originated as an image carved above the portico of the Sacred Stable of the Nikko Toshogu Shrine, a 17th-century Japanese temple. Their motto, literally translated, reads: 'Don't see, don't hear and don't speak' and is popularly rendered as: 'See no evil, hear no evil and speak no evil.'

FLUTTERING BY

Both their fluttering flight and their life cycle have undoubtedly contributed to the notion that connects butterflies with the soul. Moths, however, have more sinister connotations.

All over the world, the emergence of the butterfly from a dead-looking chrysalis is seen as a symbol of the soul leaving the body at the end of life. In some cultures the dead are believed to undergo a series of transformations before eventually coming back to life as butterflies.

Both butterflies and moths have connections with witches and bad things. Some say the butterfly is the soul of a witch, but if it can be caught at night it will not be able to re-enter her evil body and will die. Moths are still often called witches and are believed to do evil deeds during the hours of darkness. Children were traditionally encouraged to kill them with hammers or at least catch them before they could steal the miller's grain.

Both angels and fairies are often depicted with butterfly wings, as is Psyche, the beautiful maiden loved by

It is said that to dream of a butterfly represents a wish to attain perfection or freedom from life's troubles.

Shakespeare used the butterfly to illustrate human fickleness when he wrote that 'men, like butterflies/Show not their mealy wings but to the summer.'

the immortal Eros, who visited her only in the dark so she should not know who he was. Fearing that he would not let her see him because he was a hideous monster, one night she lit a lamp while he was asleep to find out what her lover looked like. But a drop of hot oil fell on him and he woke and fled. Psyche spent years a-flutter, searching for her love.

THE WISDOM OF SALMON

The salmon's long and arduous up-river journey to its spawning grounds is taken as evidence of its wisdom. This fish was once prized as the food of kings and only those of royal birth could eat it.

The Irish legend of Fionn MacCumal tells how the warrior-to-be met the poet Finneces, who taught him the lessons of life. For seven years Finneces had been trying to catch the salmon of knowledge, which lived in a pool on the river Boyne: whoever ate the salmon would gain all the knowledge in the world. Eventually he caught it, and told the boy to cook it for him. While doing so Fionn burned his thumb, which he instinctively put in his mouth, and in so doing he swallowed a piece of the salmon's skin. He thus became imbued with the salmon's wisdom and from that day could call on it simply by sucking his thumb.

In western North America, where

the salmon harvest was vital to the survival of the indigenous people, the leaping of salmon up massive rapids was explained by an earthquake, brought about by an evil spirit which, in trying to injure the people, blocked the fish's journey. The tribes of British Columbia constructed salmon 'ladders' for the fish to ascend, even resting on the rungs when exhausted. By setting salmon traps on these ledges, they could catch the fish easily.

THE SERPENT OF EVIL

Limbless, silent and deadly – it is easy to see how snakes have come to be prime symbols of evil, not least because of the role played by the serpent in the Garden of Eden.

As Genesis tells us, it was the serpent (which possessed the secrets of life) who persuaded Eve, the first woman, to eat the forbidden fruit from the tree of knowledge. As a result sin came into the world and marred what had until that moment been a state of perfection. After the event, God punished the creature, saying: 'Cursed are you above all the livestock and all the wild animals! You will crawl on your belly and you will eat dust all the days of your life.'

The snake in the grass – the lurking, unseen evil – is an image dating back to the poet Virgil.

The vanquishing of the evil serpent is a theme that recurs in many cultures and in legends such as those of Perseus and Medusa (see page 210). English legend relates how an abbess, St Hilda, rid the

In Christian art, the snake is often shown being crushed by the foot of Jesus, or at the foot of the cross signifying that Christ has triumphed over sin. It is said that there are no snakes in Ireland because they were driven out by the good deeds of St Patrick. In the game of snakes and ladders, players landing on snakes are down on their luck. Only ladders lead to the 'heaven' of victory.

Yorkshire valley of Eskdale of its snakes by driving them to the edge of a cliff, then cutting off their heads with her whip. The coiled ammonites (in fact fossilized shellfish) on the beach below are said to be the evidence of her success.

THE GOOD SERPENT

In many instances, the serpent is the embodiment of admirable attributes including healing and wisdom. It is also a symbol of eternity and almighty power.

The link between the snake and healing may derive from the snake's ability to grow and rejuvenate itself by sloughing its skin, an action often accomplished by squeezing its body between two rocks. The snake was sacred to Asclepius, the Greek god of healing, whose shrines were guarded by sacred snakes. He was said to disguise himself as a serpent before carrying out his healing arts, and he is depicted, like his Roman counterpart Aesculapius, holding a staff with a snake entwined around it – which is still the physicians' symbol.

Many African tribal people share the belief that the souls of the dead reside in snakes, which is why the creatures visit houses. For this reason milk and food are often left out for them at night.

The wisdom of serpents meant that they were believed to have prophetic powers, and they were kept in Greek temples. A snake in the temple of Athene was thought to have been kept alive by the soul of Erichthonius, a mythical king of Athens,

Because it can coil into a circle with its tail in its mouth, the snake represents eternity.

half human and half serpent, who as a child had been kept by Athene in a box. This box was guarded by the daughters of the mythical king Cecrops (meaning face with a tail), the city's founder, who had

strict instructions not to open it. They did so, however, and were so frightened that they jumped off the Acropolis to their deaths.

BEETLE POWER

The behaviour of beetles – especially the scarab beetle – gave rise to their association with creation and renewal. They were sacred to the Egyptians, who believed they had divine powers.

The scarab or dung beetle (*Scarabeus sacer*) feeds on dung, which it rolls into a ball by pushing it up a slope with its hind legs. It then makes a hole in the ground, where it lodges the ball and begins to consume it. Both males and females do this, but the female may also remove a piece from the side of the ball where she lays her eggs, leaving a 'flap' with which she covers them over. Seeing the young emerging from the ball, the Egyptians believed that new beetles were being created from the earth and, by inference, made the beetles divine, though they believed the males to be the 'creators'.

By extension, the scarab was thought to hide within itself the secret of eternal life and, as a result, images of scarabs were made and worn by the Egyptians for protection. Often heavily encrusted with jewels, these amulets were worn as pendants or rings. Most notable was the 'heart scarab',

Much to be feared is the deathwatch beetle (Xestibium rufovillosum), whose larvae chew their way through structural timbers. The nocturnal adults betray their presence by a ticking sound that is heard in the quiet of a sleepless night – such as when keeping vigil beside a sickbed – and is believed to be an omen of impending death.

The Egyptian sun god Ra was sometimes represented by a large black scarab sitting in the solar boat and rolling the sun's disk across the sky, another reference to the ball-forming habits of the scarab beetle.

which was placed on the breast of a mummified dead body and inscribed on it was a petition addressed by the dead person to his or her own heart, begging it not to bear witness against the deceased when it was weighed in judgment on the day of truth.

GENTLE DEER

Although revered for their piety, deer have long been hunted for their flesh – and for sport. According to the poets, these creatures shed tears.

The verse from Psalm 42, 'As a stag longs for flowing streams, so my soul longs for you, O God!' is central to the symbolism of the deer in Christian iconography. When shown unmoving the animal is used to portray spiritual longing, but when it is depicted drinking it represents fulfilment.

The gentleness of the deer, and its fate in the hunt, was immortalized in the 1942 Walt Disney feature length cartoon Bambi, *based on a vastly more realistic book of the same name by the German author Felix Salten (the pseudonym of Siegmund Salzmann) published in 1926.*

A stag with a crucifix between its horns is a reminder of St Hubert, heir to the dukedom of Aquitaine in the 7th century, who, in the story, was converted to Christianity when he was out hunting and saw that the deer he was about to shoot bore such an embellishment – an experience shared with St Eustace, who is often similarly represented. Hubert relinquished all his titles and wealth to enter the church.

The hunted deer may indeed produce oily secretions from its eyes, but these are not real 'tears'. However, the animal's suffering is real enough, as Shakespeare comments in *As You Like It*:

> *… a poor sequester'd stag,*
> *That from the hunter's aim had ta'en a hurt,*

Did come to languish; and indeed my lord,
The wretched animal heav'd forth such groans
That their discharge did stretch his leathern coat
Almost to bursting; and the big round tears
Cours'd one another down his innocent nose
In piteous chase ...

WORSHIPPED CATS

Since the days of ancient Egypt cats have been worshipped and revered. As well as being human companions and vermin exterminators extraordinary, many are renowned for bringing good luck.

Their natural instinct to catch and kill rats and mice is possibly the trait that first endeared cats to the ancient Egyptians, for it was the cats that kept the precious granaries free from rodent ravages. On the death of a cat, Egyptian owners would even shave their eyebrows as a mark of respect. The creature's body would be taken to Bubastis, the city of the cat-headed goddess Bast or Pasht (who was believed to have nine lives) where it was embalmed in costly spices. The Chinese, too, used cats to protect their silkworms from rats. Even images of 'silkworm cats' were thought to be effective if no live animals were to hand.

> *Freya, Scandinavian goddess of love and fertility, travelled in a chariot drawn by cats.*

> *To deliberately kill a cat was a crime in ancient Egypt that could result in the culprit's death.*

Despite their associations with evil (see next page) cats achieved high repute in medieval Europe. In 10th-century Wales Howel Dha 'the Good' ruled that the price of a kitten before it could see was a penny. If it caught a mouse its value rose to twopence. If anyone killed or stole a cat that guarded the prince's granary the offender was 'compelled either to forfeit a ewe, or as much wheat as would cover the cat when suspended by its tail'.

While black cats are lucky in Britain, elsewhere in Europe white ones have this effect. A cat with fur in three colours (as in a tabby or tortoiseshell) was once thought to provide protection against fire. And the brains of any dead cat would, it was said, have a lethal effect when fed to an enemy.

CAT CAUTIONS
Why cats need to be regarded with respect:

- *If you kick a cat it will give you rheumatism.*
- *The Devil will haunt you if you kill a cat.*
- *A cat's purr is the sound of a ghost.*
- *It is extremely unlucky for a cat to die in your house.*
- *A cat's cough will be caught by everyone in the family.*
- *Cats can suck babies' breath and kill them.*

Cats were, some say, accidentally created by the Devil, who tried to produce humans but made only cats without skins. Out of pity for the unfortunate animals, St Peter gave them their only valuable asset – fur coats.

THE BAD CAT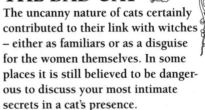

The uncanny nature of cats certainly contributed to their link with witches – either as familiars or as a disguise for the women themselves. In some places it is still believed to be dangerous to discuss your most intimate secrets in a cat's presence.

Of all the cats reviled for their evil associations, those born in May – a time of year when witchcraft was at its height – were most feared. The so-called 'May kittens' were routinely drowned at birth as they would be poor mousers and bring snakes and other unwanted creatures into the house. In Hungary, kittens, whenever born, were believed to turn into witches between the ages of seven and twelve. To prevent this transformation cuts in the shape of a cross were routinely made into the animals' skins.

To test whether or not a cat was really a witch in disguise it was an old custom to immerse the animal in holy water. If it attempted to escape (which it no doubt did) its evil nature was revealed.

CATTY HABITS

Their self-sufficiency and powerful night vision are two of the most mysterious qualities of cats. Cat lovers admire the independence of the creatures, and their penchant for doing just what they like, when they like.

Reverence for the cat, and the legend that a cat gave birth to kittens at the same moment as Christ was born, probably led to the animal's association with the Virgin Mary. Leonardo da Vinci was one of many artists who depicted a cat in scenes of the Virgin and Child.

Kipling got the nature of the cat just right in his *Just So Stories* when he described a time before the dog, the horse and the cow were domesticated and all 'the Tame animals were wild':

'But the wildest of all the wild animals was the Cat. He walked by himself, and all wild places were alike to him ... [then] the Cat went back through the Wet Wild Woods waving his wild tail and walking by his wild lone ...'

The fixed, unblinking stare of the cat adds to its mystique. What's more, cats' eyes shine in the dark and their pupils contract and dilate hugely with changes in the intensity of the light. You see a yellowish glow if you shine a light into a cat's eyes at night. Add to this their habit of hunting at night and you have an animal that is indubitably 'dark'.

THE QUOTABLE CAT

- 'A cat has absolute emotional honesty: human beings, for one reason or another may hide their feelings, but a cat does not.' (Ernest Hemingway)
- 'Cats are the ultimate narcissists. You can tell this because of all the time they spend on personal grooming …' (James Gorman)
- 'Cats know how we feel … they just don't give a damn.' (Anon)
- 'Cats are mysterious kind of folk. There is more passing in their minds than we are aware of.' (Sir Walter Scott)
- 'A cat knows you are the keys to his happiness … a man thinks he is.' (Anon)

THE FAITHFUL DOG

'Man's best friends', dogs are our companions and the guardians of our homes, appreciated for their faithfulness and trainability – the exact opposite of cats.

At the end of his story 'The Cat that Walked by Himself' Rudyard Kipling compares cats and dogs:

> *Pussy can sit by the fire and sing,*
> *Pussy can climb a tree,*
> *Or play with a silly old cork and string*
> *To 'muse herself, not me.*
> *But I like Binkie my dog, because*
> *He knows how to behave;*
> *So, Binkie's the same as the First Friend was,*
> *And I am the Man in the Cave.*

The first dogs to be tamed were probably those drawn to human settlements where they could be guaranteed at least some scraps of leftovers. Soon they were not only guarding their human companions but being used in the hunting chase – like the 'greyhound' depicted pursuing a gazelle on a piece of Mesopotamian pottery some 8000 years old.

DOGGY SAYINGS

The nature of the dog summed up by some of those who know ...

- 'The tiniest Poodle or Chihuahua is still a wolf at heart.' (Dorothy Hinshaw)
- 'To err is human, to forgive, canine.' (Anon)
- 'If you pick up a starving dog and make him prosperous, he will not bite you; that is the principal difference between a dog and a man.' (Mark Twain)

- 'Dogs have given us their absolute all. We are the center of their universe ... They serve us in return for scraps. It is without a doubt the best deal man has ever made.' (Roger Caras)
- 'The dog who barks furiously at a beggar will let a well-dressed man pass him without opposition.' (TH Huxley)

THE FEARSOME BITE, THE DREADED HOWL

The bite of a dog was, until modern times, rightly feared, for rabies was a real threat to life. Scratching, digging in undesirable places and howling were other ominous forms of behaviour.

Beware of dogs that howl in the night. These are greatly feared as omens of death, especially if they raise their voices in or near a house where someone is sick. Also to be feared in such circumstances is a dog that is driven away but comes back again. A dog seen scratching the earth was once deemed to be digging a grave.

So terrifying was the prospect of being bitten by a rabid dog that animals that howled on Christmas Eve were killed, on the supposition that such behaviour betrayed the fact that they would go mad the following year. In the Channel Island of Guernsey it was the custom to chant these words to a dog as a way of telling it not to bite:

> *The annals of superstition say that you should welcome a strange dog that enters your home voluntarily. It will keep away all troubles.*

May thy tail hang down!
May St Peter's key close thy jaws until tomorrow!

Even a bite from a perfectly healthy dog might lead to the creature being put down, following the logic that, if the animal should go mad in the future then the person bitten would, equally, become insane. In a vain attempt to effect a cure, people bitten by a rabid dog would eat the grass from a churchyard and apply to the wound dog's hair fried in oil and mixed with rosemary. Even the animal's flesh might be eaten – including the heart, after it had been dried and powdered.

THE GUARD DOG

Dogs have no doubt been helping to guard us and our property for as long as they have been our companions. Most fearsome of all was Cerberus, who kept guard at Hades' gate.

A poodle named Boye was the constant companion of Prince Rupert of the Rhine, even riding into battle draped over his master's saddle. The Puritans attacked the animal in a pamphlet, deeming him (in modern English): 'No better than a witch in the shape of a white dog' and 'A Popish, profane dog, more than half a devil, a kind of spirit.'

Writing in *The Art of Husbandry*, the 16th-century writer Conrad Heresbach (as translated by Barnaby Googe) extolled the virtues of the mastiff as a guard and watchdog: 'First the mastie [mastiff] that keepeth the house: for this purpose you must provide you such a one as hath a large and mightie body, a great and shrill voyce, that both with his barking he may discover, and with his sight dismay the theefe, yea, being not seene, with the horror of his voice put him to flight … for he is but to fight at home, and to give warning of the enemie.'

Cerberus, the many-headed guard dog of Hades, resided at the entrance to

In modern parlance a watchdog can also be a person or group appointed to monitor some aspect of public life, such as the performance and the behaviour of institutions ranging from the police force to public transport.

the underworld on the far side of the River Styx. There he prevented the souls or 'shades' of the dead from leaving; he also greeted the newly deceased as they were rowed across by Charon the ferry-man, sometimes in a friendly way, but sometimes with ferocious snarling. To ensure that he remained in an amenable mood the dead were provided with honey-cakes with which to placate the creature and keep him occupied as they passed. These so-called 'sops to Cerberus' are now used metaphorically to describe any small sweetener offered to avert a threat temporarily.

THE POWER OF PLANTS

In legend, Gaia, the Greek goddess of the earth, born from the dark space of Chaos, not only gave rise to the mountains and seas, but was responsible for the earth's green fertility. Of all the powers that plants possess, the most potent lies in the fact that they are green. For with the sun's energy and the help of the green substance chlorophyll, the plants that form the earth's green carpet ultimately create food for the myriad animals – including ourselves – that inhabit the planet.

Many plants have a most special place in our lives because they provide us with foods essential to our survival, and it is no coincidence that plants such as rice, apples and grapes are the subjects of myths and folk tales. Flowers, too, have always had a unique place in our emotions, not least for their beauty and mystery, scents and symbolism – from rosemary 'for remembrance' to the purity of the white lily. Some, such as tulips and orchids, not only epitomize the joy of gardening but have engendered torrents of human passion beyond belief. Some are celebrated in festivals, while others have the power to change our perceptions.

Though tree worship is no longer commonplace, there is still something magnificently spooky about being in the silent depths of a wood. The size and lifespan of trees links them inextricably with wisdom, curiosity and longevity, and even with the creation of the world itself. And it can surely be no coincidence that witches' broomsticks and magic wands are cut from trees, and that sticks are used to hunt for hidden treasure.

THE GREEN, GREEN GRASS

It is grass that forms the green carpets we cultivate for pleasure and recreation in our gardens, parks and sports fields. But the real bounty locked in the world's zillions of green grass blades is the food they provide.

In the 1965 ballad written by J Curly Putman the homesick prisoner longs to 'touch the green, green grass of home'. The song was a mega hit for the singer Tom Jones the following year.

Ordinary-looking grass is an extraordinary food, packed with all the nutrients that grazing animals such as cows or sheep need to stay alive. But though it is munched day and night, the grass doesn't die. That is because the growing tip of each plant lies protected beneath the surface of the soil, and there is a weak point at the base of each blade that helps ensure that the plant is not ripped out by its roots.

In Egyptian symbolism, green was the colour associated with Osiris, the god of vegetation and death.

Grass is a great food for animals, but no meal for humans. Unlike the herbivores, we don't have the right digestive equipment for breaking down and using the nutrients in blades of grass. Also, grass is toughened with sharp, hard silica (which is why it can cut). Even if we could eat it, it would quickly wear out our teeth, for unlike those of grass-eating animals they do not carry on growing as they erode.

Many grasses do not need to depend on setting seed in order to multiply, but spread themselves using underground runners (elongated stems). This is celebrated in the 19th-century poem 'The Voice of the Grass' by Sarah Roberts Boyle:

Here I come creeping, creeping everywhere
More welcome than the flowers
In summer's pleasant hours:

The gentle cow is glad,
And the merry bird not sad,
To see me creeping, creeping everywhere.

GREEN MEANINGS

- *Green is the colour of hope – every spring hope is fulfilled as the winter ends and the world turns green.*
- *In a green old age the spirit (and body) are still strong, despite advancing years.*
- *All self-respecting gardeners want green fingers.*
- *Envy is the 'green-eyed monster'.*
- *Seasickness tinges any face with a shade of green.*

THE WONDER OF WHEAT

Wheat (or corn), the 'most esteemed of cereals', is one of the most successful plants ever grown. A staple food that gives us flour – and thus bread – it is an emblem of life itself.

About 12,000 years ago, the ancients probably began to harvest wild wheats belonging to the grass genus *Triticum*. One of the first of these was *T. monococcum* or eincorn ('one-grain') wheat, which grew in Turkey. Another was emmer wheat, *T. dicoccum*, which originated in the Middle East. Although robust, emmer was not very good for bread making, but some 8000 years ago, by a lucky accident, emmer interbred naturally with another *Triticum* species. The result was *T. aestivum*, the bread wheat cultivated today in thousands of different varieties.

A story is told of an Arab lost in the desert who arrived at an oasis where, in his search for food, he came across what looked like a bag of flour. 'God be praised,' he exclaimed, 'I am saved'. He quickly untied the bag then cried: 'Alas, unfortunate wretch that I am! It is only gold dust!'

Wheat was the vital commodity that made ancient Egypt rich (thanks to the annual flooding of the Nile), and the Bible tells how, in a time of famine, Joseph was able to supply neighbouring countries with corn grown in Egypt. In Roman times grain grown in Britain and Gaul (France) was exported to Italy, and wheat arrived in the Americas when the Spanish began growing it in Mexico in 1529. As wheat farming spread northward, great forests were cleared to create the vast expanses of the American prairies.

CEREAL SAYINGS

Wheat is the subject of many proverbs and pronouncements:

- 'Unless a grain of wheat falls in the earth and dies, it remains just a single grain; but if it dies it bears much fruit.' – St John's Gospel. (Wheat is a symbol of resurrection.)
- 'He that sows good seed shall reap good corn.' (It pays to lay good foundations.)
- 'Corn and horn go together.' (Good wheat means good cattle.)

- 'Much corn lies under the straw that is not seen.' (Not all attributes are easily appreciated.)
- 'There is corn in Egypt while there is cash in Leadenhall [where the British East India Company had its headquarters].' (Charles Lamb's assertion that it was his clerk's job, rather than his writing, that would keep him solvent.)

PRECIOUS RICE GRAINS

For about half of humanity, rice is the staple food – and so important to survival that its cultivation and use is surrounded by tradition and superstition in some of the world's oldest cultures.

In China, it is a common daily greeting to say 'Have you eaten your rice?' in the way that we would say 'How are you?' In Thailand, the family is called to a meal with the words 'Eat rice'. In India, rice is the food a new bride

offers to her husband and, re-enacting an old fertility ritual, most of us will have thrown rice or its paper equivalent, confetti, over newly-weds.

Rice, the seed of the plant *Oryza sativa*, was probably first gathered at least 12,000 years ago by the Hoab-inhian people who lived in southern China and north Vietnam. As its cultivation spread, and new varieties were bred, growers discovered that while some of these thrived in the 'dry' conditions favoured by the original grass, others did best in fields flooded with shallow, slow-moving water.

Both the ancient Greeks and Romans knew about rice but regarded it as a luxurious import, more suitable for use as medicine than as food. The Moors introduced rice cultivation to Spain in the 8th century, and it spread to Italy and France during the Middle Ages.

Although rice is now widely grown in the USA it did not arrive in the Americas until the 17th century; the first successful US crops are believed to have been raised from seed brought from Madagascar. Thomas Jefferson, in his quest to discover why, in Paris, Italian rice was fetching higher prices than that from Carolina, is rumoured to have smuggled home some Italian seed to use in breeding experiments.

RICE LORE
Rituals and sayings that underline the high esteem in which rice is held.

Bali – *Rice has a soul and must be addressed as 'mother', 'grandmother' or 'grandfather'.*
China – *'Precious things are not pearls and jade but the five grains, of which rice is the finest.'*

Sri Lanka – *Prayers are said over the first rice seeds as they are sown.*
India – *'Grains of rice should be like two brothers – close but not stuck together.'*
Japan – *'Money may be squandered, but never rice.'*

POTATO LORE

Is it a cause of disease or a super food? Over the centuries the potato – a swollen tuber of the plant *Solanum tuberosum* – has not only had a fluctuating reputation but has changed the course of history.

In 1537 the Spanish invaders of Colombia became the first 'foreigners' to encounter the potato, a tuber that had been cultivated in South America for 2000 years. Small, knobbly, bitter and in various colours – including purple – primitive potatoes aroused mixed feelings in Europe. To some they were a source of strength and even an aphrodisiac. Others believed that they caused leprosy.

Prejudice persisted. Because they were not mentioned in the Bible, potatoes were rejected by Protestants as deeply unholy and 'the Devil's work'. Irish Catholics overcame the problem by sprinkling them with holy water before planting them on Good Friday. By the 1840s, the potato had become the staple of the Irish poor. When the harvest failed in both 1845 and 1846 (due to attack from potato blight, a fungal disease) over a million people died. The famine was the trigger for mass emigration to America.

> *To dispel 18th-century prejudice against the potato the French agriculturist Antoine Parmentier persuaded Queen Marie Antoinette to wear potato flowers in her corsage. Potato dishes soon became the height of fashion.*

MYSTERY MAIZE

> *In many parts of Britain, 'maize mazes' created annually in the crop fields have become popular summer holiday amusements.*

No one knows for certain how maize (confusingly also called corn) originated, but its succulent ears were so sacred as to be offered, with tobacco, as a gift to Christopher Columbus when he arrived in Cuba in 1492.

It was probably a grass called teosinte that was the ancestor of modern maize, but no one knows exactly how it was involved. Among the most 'primitive' types of maize known from archaeological digs – with about 50 small grains per cob – is one from Bat Cave, New Mexico, which is known to have been inhabited since about 4500 BC. What is certain, however, is that no maize growing today can reproduce itself without humans removing the 'seeds' from the cob and planting them.

Many Native American myths tell how maize came to exist. Typical is one that relates how Grandmother Earth gave it to humanity. She told Hare, the creator, to look at her breast, and he saw a plant growing from it. But the people did not know how to grow it, so a clan chief undertook a fast, during which the Maize Spirit appeared to him and told him all he needed to know. A female spirit is still said to live on in the tassels that appear on the corn ears.

Maize grains come in yellow, purple and even lucky red, to which Henry Wadhurst Longfellow referred: 'Then in the golden weather the maize was husked, and the maidens/Blushed at each blood-red ear, for that betokened a lover.'
It is a well-known American superstition that if a girl finds a red maize ear she will have a suitor within the year.

THE APPLE OF IMMORTALITY

It is a popular myth that Adam and Eve ate an apple in the Garden of Eden, although the Bible tells us only that they partook of 'forbidden fruit' (it was probably a fig). Apples have long been associated with immortality.

The apple tree was revered by the Druids, not only for its fruit but because it was one of the trees on which sacred mistletoe grew.

The apple features in tales from many cultures. In Scandinavia it was said that the goddess Idun was in charge of mirac-

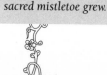

ulous apples, which, because they conferred perpetual youth, were reserved as food for the gods. But when the evil spirit Loki carried off and hid both Idun and her tree, the gods grew old and mortals fell prey to evil and sin.

The Greeks believed that Dionysus created the apple to present to Aphrodite to assure her fertility. More famous were the three golden apples that Heracles had to pluck from the tree of the Hesperides (the nymphs of the evening). They had been given by Gaia, the earth mother, to Zeus and Hera at their wedding. Hera planted them in her garden, near Mount Atlas, and sent the 100-headed monster Ladon to guard them.

> *According to superstition, an apple still hanging on a tree after winter is past foretells a death.*

APPLE WISE

The apple has been widely used as a metaphor in many aspects of life:

- *Eat an apple going to bed, make the doctor beg his bread. (Eat fruit to stay healthy.)*
- *Better an apple given than eaten. (It's better to give than to indulge yourself.)*
- *No good apple [grows] on a sour stock. (Breeding is all-important.)*

- *The apple never falls far from the tree. (A person's character always makes itself obvious.)*
- *As sure as God made little apples … (An expression of certainty.)*
- *There is small choice in rotten apples. (Bad is always bad.)*

THE HAZEL DIVINING ROD

Placed in the correct hands, a branch from a hazel (or a thorn or fruit tree) has been believed, since ancient times, to be able to summon up the secrets of the earth. This includes predicting the presence of hidden water or even buried treasure.

The original uses of the divining rod were many, including the driving out of devils, but it is best known for its ability to 'sense' underground springs. Typically, the diviner cuts a forked branch about 18in (45cm) long and grasps the prongs firmly between the thumb and two first fingers of each hand. With the joint pointing downwards, he or she walks over the ground. On encountering water, the joint in the branch will begin to rise of its own accord and when exactly over a spring will make a complete revolution, breaking or bending the twig.

The force of the twig's movement in the diviners' hands is thought to relate exactly to the depth of the spring, and also to produce a profound mental exhaustion. A certain Lady Noel was said to have 'a degree of agitation … visible in her face' as the result of the particularly rapid motion of a divining rod.

For a divining rod to have maximum potency it should, according to ancient belief, be cut between sunset and sunrise, ideally on a holy day or at new moon. If cut in the morning, it should be the branch on which the sun first shines.

The blackthorn is known in Germany as the 'wishing thorn' because of its divining powers. The Chinese traditionally chose fruit tree branches cut on the first new moon after the winter solstice.

THE PROPHETIC OAK

It was an ancient belief that trees were inhabited by gods, who not only made leaves rustle but gave them powers to foretell the future. None was more potent than the Dodona oak.

The most famous of all 'oracle trees' grew at Dodona in northwestern Greece. Here, one special tree among a grove of oaks was, from the 14th and 13th centuries BC, believed to be sacred to Zeus. Beneath it sat a bevy

A branch from the tree at Dodona is said to have been incorporated into the *Argo*, the vessel sailed in by Jason and the Argonauts on the quest for the golden fleece. Warnings from the branch kept the crew safe during their journey.

of priests, the Selloi, whose role was to interpret the rustlings of the leaves as oracular messages. (They slept on the bare ground and never washed their feet; they also translated the 'voice' of a sacred spring that welled up at the base of the tree.)

The Greek author Ovid tells of Aeacus, whose island home, Aegina, was struck by plague and famine. Sitting under an oak tree, Aeacus saw an army of ants marching past and implored Zeus: 'O most excellent father, grant me just as many subjects to fill my empty walls.' He then kissed the sacred tree, fell asleep underneath it and awoke to find that the ants had been miraculously changed into men.

THE ASH: TREE OF LIFE

Trees have always had a special place in the human heart, none more so than the gigantic ash that, in Scandinavian mythology, was thought to be the origin of all things. They named it Yggdrasil, the world tree.

Yggdrasil was 'the greatest and best of all trees'. It overshadowed the world, its topmost branches and deepest roots binding together heaven and hell. In the highest branches sat a golden cock, Vithofnir, which kept watch for the gods' enemies and crowed warnings when the Giants were threatening to attack. The gods met daily under the tree to pass judgment on mortals. Under one of the roots of Yggdrasil there was a realm of

'As straight as a white ash tree' was, in the pioneering days of America, the highest compliment that could be paid to a young man. It arose from the strength and height of the tree whose wood was used by Native Americans for making canoe paddles.

nine worlds called Niflhel, 'the hollow place', which was reserved for those who had died of old age or disease. It was guarded by the dog Garm and ruled by the goddess Hel, though unlike the Christian hell it was regarded as another world rather than a place of punishment. Beneath the other two roots were Midgard (middle earth) and Asgard, a space sacred to the gods.

> *It was an old belief that snakes will not creep over a circle of ash leaves on the ground, and that if an ash twig is used to draw a circle around a snake on the ground the creature will die of starvation.*

WAND OF WOOD – AND MAGIC

The wand – a symbol of authority – is also, in the right hands, an agent of intense psychic energy. The wood it is made of can be of great significance to its powers.

> *In the Bible, Aaron's rod exerted its miraculous powers during the plagues that preceded the Exodus, and the rod of Moses was used to part the Red Sea. Even removed from Aaron's grasp, his rod retained its powers. It not only swallowed the rods of the Egyptian magicians, but also blossomed and bore fruit in the Tabernacle, confirming the exclusive rights to the priesthood of the tribe of Levi.*

The cutting and shaping of a wizard's magic wand was carried out in great secrecy, with prayers offered to give the rod both power and authority. The knife used would have been baptized in blood. Hazel was a favourite wood (usually a branch was cut at sunrise to endow it with maximum solar energy), but the Druids often also chose sacred trees such as yew, hawthorn and rowan.

If they wished to communicate with Satan, witches would choose a wand of cypress (the tree of death) and, at midnight, draw a circle on the ground at a crossroads. Witches also used wands (elder was another favourite wood) to locate buried treasure, to test girls' virginity and to identify murderers, thieves and other criminals.

THE FLYING BROOMSTICK

Astride her broomstick, the witch is pictured flying through the sky – out and about to work her evil. The broomstick's powers were ensured by the application of flying ointment.

It was the custom, at their initiation, for apprentice witches to be presented with flying sticks, commonly known as broomsticks. In 1563 one Martin Tuloff of Guernsey reported seeing his mother sit astride her broomstick and disappear up the chimney chanting: 'Go in the name of the Devil and Lucifer over rocks and thorns.'

The 'flying ointment' with which the women daubed their broomsticks may have contained ergot, a poisonous fungus found on rye, which would produce powerful hallucinogenic effects when absorbed through the skin.

Alice Kyteler, a famous Irish witch of the 14th century, was one of the first to be described riding on a broomstick. On it she reputedly 'ambled through thick and thin, when and in what manner she listed, after having greased it with ointment which was found in her possession'. Though accused of murdering three husbands as well as practising witchcraft, she escaped to England – and was never tried.

The old custom of pushing a broom up the chimney as a sign that a housewife was not in residence may have led to the idea that witches flew up the chimney on their broomsticks.

WITCHES' PLANTS

Many plants are associated with the power that witches can exert – and also with breaking their spells. Evil hags prized those plants they believed could help them carry out their magic and mayhem.

Most mysterious of all witches' plants is the mandrake (*Mandragora officinarum*) whose root looks like a human body. When dug up (this had to be done by a dog, as the plant could strike a person dead on the spot) it would, in the right hands, whisper the whereabouts of hidden treasure and foretell the future. Witches also used mandrake root for everything from controlling fertility to curing the dying.

Oranges were employed in witchcraft until at least the 1880s to represent the heart of an intended victim. The unfortunate person's name was written on a piece of paper, which was attached to the fruit using many pins and placed in the chimney until the victim died.

Following witch lore, parents anxious that a daughter might have lost her virginity would feed her powdered yellow lily. If still a virgin she would at once experience the urge to urinate.

BRANCHES OF THE GALLOWS TREE

While Christians speak of 'the tree' as the cross on which Jesus was crucified, the branches of trees have long been the site of executions – both just and unjust.

In Germany, trials once commonly took place under lime (linden) trees, which were then used to hang the guilty. An ancient lime tree that still grows at Schenklengsfeld in central Germany served such a purpose, but is also a symbol of love and fertility.

An oak growing northeast of Grandview, Texas, was described by Edward Riley, a witness to 'frontier justice', as growing 'in a slanting position' and having 'one special limb [that] extends out in a straight level with the ground'. Here, said Riley, during a two-year period, 11 hangings took place – the result of 55 trials – in the 1870s.

The use of a tree as a gallows is poignantly described by Oscar Wilde in *The Ballad of Reading Gaol*:

For oak and elm have pleasant leaves
That in the spring-time shoot:
But grim to see is the gallows-tree,
With its adder-bitten root,

And, green or dry, a man must die
Before it bears its fruit!

NAMES AND STORIES

- *The role of trees as gallows lives on in names such as the Hanged Man Tree and the Gibbet Oak.*
- *According to medieval legend, the cross on which Christ died was made from wood from the Tree of Life.*
- *If a dog is afraid to approach a tree, so it's said in the Southern USA, it is one on which a man was once hanged.*
- *The Judas tree (Cercis spp) with deep purple-red flowers, is so named because it is said to be the tree on which Christ's betrayer, Judas Iscariot, hanged himself.*

TREES OF WISDOM AND CURIOSITY

The association of trees with wisdom and knowledge is common to many cultures and religions – a fact closely associated with their size and longevity.

Above all others the tree revered by Buddhists is the bo tree, under which Gautama sat, facing east. There he stayed, without stirring, until he had attained both knowledge and nirvana, the state of perfection, at which moment the tree shed all its leaves before growing completely new foliage. While he sat there, he was assailed with the darts of demons, and with rain, floods and hurricanes.

The sacred cedars of Lebanon are still a place of pilgrimage; at a chapel erected among the most ancient trees they are blessed in a Feast of the Cedars held every August.

The sycamore is the symbol of curiosity because of

the Biblical story of Zaccheus who, in order to obtain a better view of Jesus, climbed up such a tree. This was not, however, a sycamore with key-like fruits but a sycamore fig (*Ficus sycomorus*), with a mulberry-like leaf and fruits like figs. The ancients dubbed it 'the wisest of trees' because it comes into bud late in spring and therefore avoids the frost.

The Tolawa people of Pacific North America greatly revere the giant redwood. They believe that when the world was created, such a tree stood at its centre, and that beneath it could be seen the tracks of all the animals the creator had made.

THE MYSTERIOUS UPSIDE-DOWN TREE

With its gigantic girth and grizzled root-like branches with their meagre covering of leaves, the baobab is aptly named the upside-down tree. Many myths and legends surround this African 'tree of life'.

It is not only its odd appearance that makes the baobab (*Adansonia digitata*) special. During each rainy season its massive trunk, measuring up to 60ft (18m) in circumference, absorbs up to 30,000 gallons (136,000 litres) of water. This not only keeps the tree alive but also sustains Kalahari bushmen who, among others, have learned how to suck out the precious liquid through hollow grass stems.

So how did the baobab come to look so strange? One story is that after God created the baobab, the tree looked at his reflection in a pond and disliked what he saw. Hearing his complaints, God asked him if he found the hippopotamus beautiful, and whether he liked the hyena's cry. But the tree kept on complaining, so God came down to earth, uprooted the tree and replanted him upside down.

> *Beware of plucking the flowers of a baobab. Not only are they inhabited by spirits but anyone taking a flower will, it's said, be eaten by a lion.*

THE IMMORTAL OLIVE

The olive, symbol of peace, was sacred to the ancient Greeks. It appears in many Biblical stories, from the Flood to the Crucifixion.

'The murmur of an olive grove,' wrote Vincent van Gogh, who painted 19 pictures featuring olive trees, 'has something very intimate, immensely old …' Indeed, olives are among Europe's longest-lived trees, enduring for at least 1500 years, hence their reputation for 'immortality'. So ancient are many olives that there may even be trees alive today that witnessed Christ and his disciples praying in the Garden of Gethsemane at the foot of the Mount of Olives.

Athene, the goddess of wisdom, so Greek myth relates, created the olive tree by striking the rock of the Acropolis with her spear. The olive was so venerated that its image appeared on Athenian coins.

Long before, as the Old Testament recounts, the dove that Noah sent out from the Ark to test whether or not the waters of the great Flood had subsided came back with 'an olive leaf plucked off, so Noah knew that that the waters were abated.' Ever since, the olive branch has been a symbol of peace and friendship. The kings of

the Old Testament – and beyond – were anointed with
olive oil as a token of honour and divine blessing.

MORE OLIVE LEGENDS

- *The club carried by Heracles was made of olive wood
  (though some say it was cypress).*
- *To ensure a good harvest in the coming year,
  the Greeks burnt an olive branch at their
  harvest thanksgiving.*
- *When Adam died, he gave the seed of the olive
  (with those of cedar and cypress) to his son Seth.
  These were placed in the corpse's mouth and from
  it grew a triple-trunked tree.*

DEADLY INSECT-EATERS

**When the going gets tough, especially where the
soil is poor, plants resort to extraordinary means of
survival – none more so than the carnivorous plants,
which supplement their diets by trapping and digesting insects.**

The sundews (*Drosera* spp), found in Europe and as
far apart as New Zealand and Alaska, are aptly named.
When the sun shines on them liquid drops exuded from
the reddish 'tentacles' that fringe the fleshy leaves do,
indeed, sparkle like dew. But these drops do not
evaporate in the sun's heat. Lured by
their lustre, insects become trapped
and are dissolved and digested – so
upping the plant's nitrogen intake.

The eastern USA is the home of the
best known of all carnivorous plants,
the Venus flytrap (*Dionaea muscipula*),

In Little Shop of
Horrors *Audrey II is a
giant Venus flytrap with
a taste for snacking on
humans.*

named for the goddess believed to have risen from the ocean in the shell of a clam – whose shape is very similar to the plant's hinged leaves. These, arrayed with overlapping teeth, snap shut when an insect lands on them. The 'prey' cannot escape and is slowly digested.

Pitcher plants, found in the tropical forests of Asia and the Americas, attract insects with their honey-like smell. But the creatures quickly fall over the rim and into a vat of digestive liquid, and the pitcher's walls are so steep that climbing out is impossible.

> *All over Europe the sundew plant was once mixed with spices and mashed to make a liquor called* ros solis, *which was sold as an elixir of youth, hence the plant's alternative name of youthwort. In some places it is employed as a love charm.*

FLOWER 'MANIA'

Can flowers drive one mad? Not exactly, but the fever for acquiring both tulips and orchids has raged at different times in garden history.

In Holland in the 1630s it was as much a love of gambling as a love of tulips that produced what has been described as 'one of the most singular manias that has ever deranged the human mind'. A single bulb of the tulip 'Semper Augustus' was said to have sold for as much as 5500 guilders – twice the annual income of a successful merchant. Rich men were reduced to poverty when the crash came in 1637.

> *In Alexandre Dumas' novel* The Black Tulip, *the 17th-century tulip fancier Cornelius van Baerle wins a prize of 100,000 guilders for growing the elusive flower.*

One tale of the time relates how a sailor mistook a tulip bulb he found in a merchant's counting house for an onion. He took it to eat with his evening herring. The merchant, realizing what had happened, rushed to the sailor's house, only to arrive just as he was finishing his meal. For his crime the sailor was sentenced to six months in prison.

Orchids were esteemed and grown by the Chinese at least 2500 years ago. In the *I Ching* or *Book of Changes*, thought to have been edited and annotated by Confucius, is the pronouncement, 'Words by friends with one and the same heart are just as sweet as the aroma of the orchid.' The passion for orchid collecting in Europe and the USA began in the 1830s, when more than 300 species were brought from the tropics for cultivation. Though the craze was not as rampant as 'tulipomania', by the 1890s plants were exchanging hands in Britain for some 1500 guineas apiece.

CHERRY BLOSSOM BEAUTY

The beauty of spring cherry blossom is most highly appreciated by the Japanese. Their custom of celebrating the spring by viewing the blossoms is now also popular in other parts of the world, including Boston and Seattle.

'It's cherry pink and apple blossom white/ When your true lover comes your way' are the opening lyrics of a song that was very popular in the 1950s. The most famous, instrumental, version by Perez Prado reached the top of the US Billboard charts in 1955.

Honouring the spring blossoms, the celebration called *hanami* is a ritual that goes back centuries, though only since the Heian period (794–1185) has cherry blossom been its focus (before then it centred on the Japanese apricot). It was a religious occasion, at which the aristocracy would celebrate with lavish picnics under trees and the cherry blossoms were likened to a bumper harvest of rice. Today it is a secular occasion enjoyed by all.

In the 8th century people would climb Mount

Tsukuba to sing and dance among the flowers. Both in the Japanese warrior tradition, and in Buddhism, the brief beauty of the cherry blossoms became symbolic of power. The 16th-century warlord Toyotomi Hideyoshi, for instance, held grand *hanami* as a way of flaunting his authority. The cherry blossom is now considered to be Japan's national flower.

From late March, Japanese meteorologists report daily on the northward movement of the 'cherry blossom front' or *sakura zensen*, the warm front that ends the winter and heralds the blossom. Because its arrival is unpredictable, and the blossoms short-lived, the saying goes: 'If there were no cherry blossoms in this world, how much more tranquil our hearts would be in spring'.

VICTORY BAY AND PALM

Both the bay (or bay laurel) branch and the palm frond are ancient symbols of victory. At the Athens Olympics in 2004 the tradition of crowning the winners with laurel wreaths was ceremoniously revive at medal presentations.

Not exactly a victory medal, but a symbol of achievement, a pilgrim returning from the Holy Land was customarily presented with a palm branch to carry home to lay on the altar of his parish church, hence the name 'palmer' was used for a pilgrim.

A crown of laurel (*Laurus nobilis*) was the coveted prize awarded in ancient Greece at the Pythian games, held at Delphi in honour of Apollo, god of poetry and song (and named for the god's purification by python's blood). Because these included performances by poets, orators and philosophers, the bay has come to symbolize excellence in the arts.

For the Romans, laurel was a victory symbol, used as a wrapping for the dispatches of generals (and as wreaths for the victorious), and as decoration for soldiers' weapons. Pliny says that it was forbidden to 'pollute the laurel' and that it 'must not be employed even for making a fire at altars and shrines when divinities are to be propitiated'.

The palm gets its name from the likeness of its leaf to the spread palm of the hand. Its association with victory comes from the stature of the tree and the fact that it is evergreen. In Roman times, fronds were carried in triumphal processions and awarded to victorious gladiators. Christians adopted the palm as a symbol of victory over death – and entry into heaven – especially by martyrdom, because Jesus, entering Jerusalem, was feted by a crowd waving palm branches and crying 'Hosanna'.

LAUREL MYTHS AND BELIEFS

- *A laurel wreath on the door will prevent disease from entering a house.*
- *A laurel leaf put under the pillow at night will inspire the would-be poet.*
- *The death of a bay tree is an omen of disaster.*
- *Wearing laurel leaves will avert the plague.*
- *Keeping a bay leaf in the mouth all day will avert misfortune.*

FACES TO THE SUN

A field of sunflowers, heads all turned resolutely to the sun, is a remarkable sight. Famous as subjects of Van Gogh's paintings, these flowers are the object of both admiration and myth.

As a punishment for betraying him, the fickle sun god Helios transformed his first love, the sea nymph Clytie, into a sunflower. In remembrance of their love she turns her head, in gratitude, towards the sun. So myth explains the habits of sunflowers (*Helianthus* spp) – and marigolds, for it was probably the marigold, *Calendula officinalis*, which grows wild all over Europe, that was really the flower of this story.

The large sunflower we now grow was brought to Europe by the Spanish from South America, where for centuries the Incas worshipped it as an incarnation of the sun and ate its seeds in religious ceremonies. Priestesses of the sun wore sunflowers made of 'virgin gold' on their breasts and as crowns on their heads.

In praise of the sunflower, Erasmus Darwin, the grandfather of Charles, wrote that it:

Climbs the upland lawn,
And bows in homage to the rising dawn,
Imbibes with eagle eye the golden ray,
And watches, as it moves, the orb of day.

THE USEFUL COCONUT

Dubbed the world's most useful tree, the coconut provides drink, food (and a bowl to eat it from), plus material for building homes and thatching roofs.

Where the coconut came from is a matter of speculation. The majority view, backed by its mention in Indian documents over 2000 years old, is that it originates from eastern Asia. Some people maintain that early Spanish invaders discovered it growing in Panama. The palm has become one of the world's most important crops, especially for its yield of copra – the dried coconut flesh from which oil is pressed.

Occasionally, 'pearls' are said to form inside a coconut, possibly as a result of defective germination. Composed of calcium carbonate, and remarkably like oyster pearls, white or with a bluish tinge, they can grow as big as cherries. In his *Herbarium Amboinensis*, the 17th-century German naturalist Georg Eberhard Rumphius described and illustrated some exquisite examples, often mounted in gold and silver, owned by Malay dynasties.

COCONUT TRADITIONS
The coconut features in many customs:

Parsee – *Breaking a coconut on the threshold is the best welcome to a new bride and groom.*

Western India – *Throwing coconut and flowers into the sea on one day each year is the thanks needed to tame the ocean.*

Senegal – *A coconut will only fall on the head of someone who has aroused the displeasure of the gods.*

Fiji – *Spin a coconut near a sick person. If it falls towards the east they will recover.*

Sri Lanka – *The first coconut grew from the head of a slain monster.*

TOBACCO SMOKE – WAFTING UP TO HEAVEN

Smoking tobacco was once a ritual used to propitiate the gods, though today anyone trying to break the smoking habit might consider it to be more of a curse than a blessing.

Using leaves stuffed into hollow reeds, or rolled into cylinders (the original cigars) Amerindians created the smoke that carried their prayers up to the sky, the home of the gods. So began the tradition of tobacco smoking. On special occasions, a ceremonial pipe was passed between chiefs

The word cigar probably comes from the Maya word sik'ar, *which means 'smoking'.*

and warriors, or smoke was blown on to an altar, or over a magical object to bring good luck. Tobacco was also put on graves, together with other gifts, to ensure the well-being of a dead person in the afterlife.

When Columbus and his men landed in Cuba in 1492 they were amazed to see cigars being smoked. 'The effect,' said one of the first European explorers to try the leaf himself, 'is a certain drowsiness of the whole body accompanied by a certain species of intoxication ...' Indeed, the Spanish who experienced the effects of tobacco in the following century named it from the Arabic *tabaq*, meaning 'euphoria-inducing herb'. After it was brought to Europe from Florida in the 1560s, tobacco was used as everything from an aphrodisiac to a hangover cure.

> *Traditionally, tobacco has also been chewed or taken direct into the nose as snuff (ready-grated tobacco). In the late 19th and early 20th centuries in the USA, chewing tobacco was so widespread a habit that saloons and hotel lobbies provided spittoons (cuspidors) for the purpose.*

MODESTY AND CHASTITY: FLORAL VIRTUES

Flowers and leaves represent some old-fashioned virtues, in symbolism stemming from the Bible or from age-old perceptions of the plants.

'Shrinking violets' are the flowers of modesty, eulogized by the 19th-century poet John Moultrie:

> *Under the green hedges after the snow,*
> *There do the dear little violets grow,*
> *Hiding their modest and beautiful heads*
> *Under the hawthorn in soft mossy beds.*

The violet's nature had, however, been noted centuries before. Christians believed it drooped its head so demurely because the shadow of the Cross fell on it. To the Romans, violets were maidens turned purple by the bruises inflicted on them by the jealous goddess Venus and then transformed into flowers by Cupid.

After Adam and Eve had transgressed against God's instructions, and eaten the forbidden fruit, the extent of their trouble dawned upon them. As Genesis says: 'Then the eyes of both of them were opened, and they knew that they were naked; so they stitched fig-leaves together and made themselves loincloths.' Ever since, the fig leaf has been employed as a token of modesty (or prudishness), though its use in art was particularly prevalent during the Victorian era.

PLANTS OF MEMORY

Rosemary and the aptly named forget-me-not are the plants of memory. As well as being used at funerals, the evergreen rosemary was, with the holly, once widely employed for Christmas decorations.

'There's rosemary, that's for remembrance; pray, love remember,' so says Ophelia to Laertes in Shakespeare's play *Hamlet*. Sir Thomas More wrote of letting the plant 'run all over my garden wall, not only because my bees love it, but because it is the herb sacred to remembrance, and therefore to friendship'. How the link came about is not known, but some speculate that it is because rosemary (*Rosmarinus*) has such a lingering scent, and smells can so easily evoke vivid memories.

It is said that after the battle of Waterloo, whole fields of forget-me-nots sprang up on the ground where men had been slaughtered, the soil having been enriched by the blood of heroes.

The forget-me-not (*Myosotis*), dubbed by the poet Samuel Taylor Coleridge 'hope's gentle gem', got its common name, so a German legend relates, when a knight's fiancée espied the flower floating down the Danube and wanted to possess it. Her gallant partner jumped into the water and grasped the plant with its bright blue flowers but, encumbered by his armour, was unable to get back on to land and drowned. His dying words to his lady were, 'Forget me not.'

THE WILD WOOD

As humans have tamed the landscape, they have cleared away vast areas of woodland, but surviving stands of great trees can still evoke feelings of awe.

The Wild Wood, home of Badger and other creatures in Kenneth Grahame's The Wind in the Willows, *was based on a real wood near Fowey in Cornwall. The story was originally told in letters to Grahame's son 'Mouse'.*

Danger once lurked in the forest, the home of wild creatures and a dark, forbidding place to be feared for its spirits and unseen terrors. The word 'savage' comes from the Latin *silva*, a wood. The ancients believed that the trees themselves possessed souls.

The ancient Celtic Druids, inspired by religious awe, worshipped in 'sacred groves', but the early Christians disapproved of the notion of 'holy' trees. Many ancient yew trees, however, are roughly contemporary with the medieval churches they stand beside.

As forests were gradually cut down to create farmland and build villages and towns, woodland came to be more highly valued economically (for its timber), and also aesthetically. The 18th-century essayist and headmaster Vicesimus Knox even declared that he pitied a man who could not fall in love with a tree. In the Romantic period, woods became places for retreat and contemplation.

THE PRECIOUS VINE

The vine and its fruit are ancient symbols of sanctity and fertility. They have resonance for Christians because of their association with the preaching and death of Jesus.

No one knows who first harvested grapes from the vine – or how and when the secrets of wine making were first discovered – but the wild grape, *Vitis vinifera*, certainly flourished in the Zagros Mountains (now in Iran) more than 7000 years ago. The Greeks, who so loved the vine that it became sacred to the god Dionysus, planted grapes in southern France around 600 BC.

The Romans carried on the tradition, and Pliny extols the vine as Italy's great asset, with which 'she can be thought to have surpassed all the blessings of the world ...' He also talks of the great size to which vines can grow, and mentions a

The twining growth of the grapevine is a metaphor for gossip, never better described than in the 1967 Barrett Strong and Norman Whitfield song 'I Heard It Through the Grapevine', first recorded by Smokey Robinson and the Miracles.

statue of Jupiter carved from a single vine stem.

For the people of the Old Testament, the vine symbolized God's blessing on his chosen people. For them it was the tree of life. Because Jesus likened himself to it, saying 'I am the vine; you are the branches', early Christians used the vine as a symbol of their faith, representing it in mosaics, wall paintings and in Rome's maze of catacombs. Grapes themselves are symbols of salvation as they produce the wine that, in the Eucharist, becomes the blood of Christ.

PAINTING WITH PLANTS

Whether to scare enemies, to render themselves attractive or to bring good fortune, people have made excellent use of vegetable dyes extracted from plants to paint their skins.

'All the Britons do colour themselves in Woad, which giveth a blew colour,' writes John Gerard in his *Herbal*, quoting an extract from Julius Caesar's account of his campaign in Britain. He also quotes Pliny with reference to this ancient British practice: 'In France they call it Glastum, which is like unto Plantaine, wherewith the British wives and their daughters are coloured all over, and go naked in some kinde of sacrifices.'

Woad (*Isatis tinctoria*) is a yellow-flowered brassica brought by incomers from southern Europe. It was grown in England for centuries and widely used

The broom plant popularly known as dyer's greenweed (Genista tinctoria) is another ancient source of dye. Its yellow pigment was traditionally mixed with woad to produce green, hence its name.

as a dye. Extracting the blue colour involved a series of fermentations, which created such a foul smell that Elizabeth I insisted that production should temporarily cease in any town she happened to be visiting.

On the other side of the world, in India, Africa and the Middle East, *mehndi*, the art of henna painting, has long been used at weddings and other celebrations, as it is believed to bring love and good fortune. A paste made of the crushed leaves of the henna plant (*Lawsonia inermis*) is applied to the skin in beautiful patterns that gradually fade. Ancient murals in caves near Mumbai (Bombay), said to date from around 350 CE, show a princess under a tree having her hands and feet painted with flower designs. A beneficial 'side effect' of henna is that it cools the skin, especially when applied to the palms of the hands and soles of the feet.

THE LANGUAGE OF FLOWERS

In the language of flowers, passion has a great many emblems, each subtly different from the next. Assigning such meanings to flowers was hugely popular in the 19th century.

According to one legend, the carnation, a type of pink (*Dianthus*) sprang to life when Christ was born. In another, it arose from the tears that his mother Mary shed when he died. Either way, this fragrant bloom has become the symbol of pure, enduring love. To the Romans it was *flos Jovis* – Jove's (Jupiter's) flower. As well as being appreciated for its colour and scent, the carnation was used to flavour food and drinks.

The evening primrose (*Oenothera*) became the emblem of silent love because of its habit of opening its delicate pale yellow petals only at night. These lines by the 19th-century poet John Clare perfectly describe it:

> *When once the sun sinks in the west,*
> *And dew-drops pearl the Evening's breast;*
> *Almost as pale as moonbeams are,*
> *Or its companionable star,*
> *The Evening Primrose opes anew*
> *Its delicate blossoms to the dew;*
> *And hermit-like, shunning the light,*
> *Wastes its fair bloom upon the night.*

As well as roses, red tulips and red chrysanthemums are also unspoken declarations of love. Red poppies, however, mean: 'My heart cannot be stormed; you must lay siege to it and be patient.'

LOVE'S BLOOMS
Many other flowers speak the language of love:

Purple lilac – *'You are my first love.'*
Primrose – *'I might learn to love you.'*
Narcissus – *'You love no one better than yourself.'*
Periwinkle –*'My heart was whole until I saw you.'*

Yellow acacia – *'Our love is secret.'*
Arbutus – *'You alone are my love.'*
Honeysuckle – *'This is a token of my love.'*
Scabious – *'You are mistaken, I do not love you.'*

THE ROSE OF LOVE

Of all the blooms in the world's flora, it is the rose, especially the red one, that speaks loudest and longest of love. It is said to have acquired its thorns only when Adam and Eve were expelled from the Garden of Eden.

The rose has always been appreciated for its beauty

and scent. Though originally a symbol of joy, secrecy and silence, it has been linked with love for at least 4000 years. The Romans were besotted with it, strewing their streets, houses and beds with petals and identifying the rose with goddesses of love Aphrodite and Venus.

Later, in the age of chivalry, knights competing in tournaments would wear roses 'as an emblem that gentleness should accompany courage, and that beauty was the reward of valour'. In the Middle Ages, the heads of a bride and her wedding guests would be adorned with delicate chaplets (rings) of roses. A chaplet of roses is still a fitting adornment for a bride – once bride-grooms wore them as well.

As a symbol of love, both won and lost, the rose is immortalized in verse, including these all-encompassing lines from Mrs Hemans:

> How much of memory dwells amidst thy bloom,
> Rose! Ever wearing beauty for thy dower!
> The bridal day – the festival – the tomb –
> Thou hast thy part in each, thou stateliest flower!

LIKE A RED, RED ROSE
Legend has it that:

- *The white rose blushed with pleasure when kissed by Eve.*
- *Venus pricked her feet and shed blood on the rose as she searched for her lover Adonis.*
- *White roses were stained red when Cupid tipped wine over them.*
- *The red hue is the blood of a nightingale, which, lovelorn for the flower, pressed its breast against the thorns.*

FLOWERS AND THEIR MEANINGS

Whether they link to a date, or need to convey a message, it is possible to find the right flower for every occasion if you know the language of flowers.

Named from 'poesy', originally a love motto or poem, the posy of flowers has long been a symbol of love, but the Victorians took the concept further, with bouquets that imparted specific sentiments. Much of their inspiration came from the East 'where all was symbol, emblem and allegory', and 'token flowers' were known as a salaam or greeting. The French also valued the floral message.

Any lady conversant with the language of flowers would be thrilled to receive a bouquet containing plum blossom ('keep your promise'), sweet pea ('meeting'), convolvulus ('night') and forget-me-not, conveying the message, 'Keep your promise, meet me tonight, do not forget.'

> The American poet James Gates Percival described the matching of flowers and sentiments:
> 'In Eastern Lands they talk in flowers,/And they tell in a garland their loves and cares:/ Each blossom that blooms in their garden bowers,/On its leaves a mystic language bears.

RIGHT FLOWER, RIGHT MONTH

Match up a floral gift or greetings card using:

January – carnation
February – primrose, violet
March – daffodil, narcissus
April – daisy
May – lily of the valley
June – rose, honeysuckle

July – water lily
August – gladiolus, poppy
September – aster
October – dahlia, cosmos
November – chrysanthemum
December – holly

FLOWERS ARRANGED

Ikebana, the Japanese art of arranging flowers, uses plants to convey specific sentiments. Modern exponents of the art have added greatly to its creativity.

Ikebana began, it is thought, when Buddhist monks, newly arrived in Japan around 540 CE, began to use flower arrangements to decorate their temples. By the 13th century it had become fashionable to create *tokonomas*, sacred alcoves containing a flower arrangement, incense and a candle, but it was not until the late 1500s that arrangements became complex, formal and meaningful.

The truly 'original' Ikebana school was Ikebono, named for the master arranger Ikebono Sengyo. Its *rikka* style of standing flowers, used for formal and ceremonial occasions, was a Buddhist expression of the beauty of nature. Seven 'branches' were created in the arrangement to represent hills, waterfalls, valleys and other features of the landscape. Pine cones symbolized rocks and stones, and white chrysanthemums a small stream.

Later, a simpler style called *shokai* developed, using three main branches. A freer style, named *nageire*, meaning 'to throw' or 'to fling in', originated as part of the tea ceremony. The *moribana* style uses flowers piled up in a shallow, flat container. Today's modern, freer and more expressive Ikebana owes much to the creative genius of Sofu Teshigahara, born in 1900.

Three essentials of Ikebana:

1 Any natural material may be used in an arrangement – fresh or withered leaves, branches, grass, stems, pods and buds (which will open and allow the arrangement to evolve).

2 A composition traditionally comprises primary, secondary and tertiary features. The primary grouping sits upright in the centre, the secondary grouping leans away from the first, the tertiary grouping leans away from the centre on the opposite side. These lines symbolize ten (heaven), jin *(humanity) and* chi *(earth) respectively.*

3 The container is an important sculptural element, and intrinsic to the composition.

PLANTS THAT TELL THE TIME

As well as opening at different seasons, plants can even tell the time. Carolus Linnaeus the 18th-century Swedish naturalist designed a famous floral clock.

As any gardener knows, flowers respond to nature's rhythms, thanks to their ability to sense changes in day length. So it is that autumn flowers, like Michaelmas daisies and chrysanthemums, open when the days are getting shorter, but spring flowers such as primroses and camellias sense the increasing hours of sunshine. Even from day to day, the petals of various flowers open and shut at specific hours – again a result of their ability to sense the changing quality of the light. Linnaeus timed the movements of some of these flowers precisely, and based his floral clock on them.

THE FLORAL CLOCK

Linnaeus's plants included the following species.
(Botanical names are current, times GMT.)

Flower	Opening time	Closing time
Goat's beard (Tragopogon pratensis)	3.00 am	9.00 am
Hawkweed/Bristly oxtongue (Picris echioides)	4.00 am	12.00 noon
Naked-stalked poppy (Papaver nudicaulis)	5.00 am	7.00 am
Smooth sow thistle (Sonchus oleraceus)	5.00 am	11.15 am
Spotted cat's ear (Hypochaeris maculata)	6.00 am	4.00 pm
African marigold (Tagetes erecta)	7.00 am	3.00 pm
Mouse-ear hawkweed (Heiracium pilosella)	8.00 am	2.00 pm
Field marigold (Calendula arvensis)	9.00 am	3.00 pm
Proliferous pink (Petrorhagia prolifera)	8.00 am	1.00 pm
Creeping mallow (Malva caroliniana)	9.15 am	12.00 noon
Chickweed (Stellaria media)	9.15 am	9.15 pm

PETAL POWER

The fabulous scents of flowers are part of nature's plan to ensure their reproduction. For us their scent is also an allure, a kind of 'love magic', especially powerful when exquisite aromas are concentrated and mixed into perfumes.

Plant perfumes do, in fact, affect the brain, influencing the areas involved with feelings of love, compassion and physical attraction. Scents can boost the libido, as men and women discovered for themselves, long before the physiologists came up with the proof.

Favoured perfumes of the past were mostly spicy, like myrrh (see page 101), until the Romans (literally) fell in love with floral scents. A Roman nobleman would have used different plant perfumes on different parts of his body, including mint for the arms, marjoram for the hair and eyebrows and essence of ivy for the neck and knees.

Arab traders probably reintroduced plant perfumes to Europe in the 16th century, since when a huge industry has developed. This origin explains why, for Shakespeare's Lady Macbeth 'all the perfumes of Arabia' could not 'sweeten' the hand that had murdered King Duncan.

In the realm of magic, the strong smells of plants like fennel, mullein, hemlock and the like are believed to have a powerful effect on demons. And it is believed that at witches' sabbaths altered states of consciousness can be brought about by anointing the body with aromatic oils. The essences of some plants could even, it was once said, make people believe that they were the human embodiment of wolves.

Famously fragrant: *Taking his cues from ancient Roman practices, the Emperor Napoleon bathed his head in eau de cologne before setting off to war, while the court of King Louis XV was dubbed 'le court parfumée' from the habit of his entourage of sprinkling perfumes liberally on their clothes and furniture as well as on their skins*

LIQUID ROSES
Of all floral scents, roses are arguably the sweetest. From emperors to ordinary mortals, they have captured countless hearts.

Rose perfume obsessions are well documented in history. The Emperor Nero spent a fortune on roses for his festivities, at which petals poured down on the guests and the fountains spouted rose water. It is said that the 9th-century Abbasid caliph Al-Mutawakkil loved the perfume of roses so much that he declared: 'I am the king of sultans and the rose is the king of the sweet scented flowers; each of us is therefore worthy of the other.'

A pot pourri of rose petals, often mixed with petals and leaves from other plants, was the Elizabethans' way of disguising foul smells.

Different types of roses give subtle differences to the final perfume. Though Alba and Centifolia roses are both valued today, traditionally the rose most favoured is Damascena, the damask rose, named from Damascus, its centre of cultivation in the 8th and 9th centuries. An 'attar' is the name for a perfume made from the petals of flowers. It takes 227lb (500kg) of rose petals to make just 15oz (500g) of concentrated perfume.

PRACTICAL PERFUMES
The Victorian housewife used rose petals for many purposes:

Scented candles – *petals mixed with wax.*

Cake decoration – *crystallized rose petals.*

Linen cupboard – *dried rose petals placed in bags.*

Sugar – *mixed with powdered petals and added to cakes and confections.*

Lozenges – *rose-flavoured to sweeten the breath.*

Jams and jellies – *made with roses for a delicate flavour.*

Rose petal vinegar – *used as a soothing compress to relieve headaches.*

THE GARDEN OF DELIGHTS

The plants we love give us the greatest pleasure when they are planted together in a garden. The original ideal of the garden was an enclosed space that contained water, trees and flowers.

'And the Lord God planted a garden eastward, in Eden … And out of the ground made the Lord God to grow every tree that is pleasant to the sight, and good for food …' So says Genesis, thus underlining the link between the garden and perfection. Indeed the original idea of Paradise is said to have been such a garden, a concept we owe to the Persians from their *pairi-daeza* – gardens whose terraced parks were most beautifully planted with flowers, shrubs and trees.

In the Hanging Gardens of Babylon, one of the seven wonders of the ancient world, the Persians of the 6th century BC created a sumptuous space in which, according to the Greek writer Diodorus, '… the several parts of the structure rose from one another tier upon tier'.

The oldest gardens we know of were those cultivated by the Egyptians in the 2nd millennium BC and depicted in their tomb paintings. The power of the garden to inspire is expressed in this love poem inscribed by a young girl on a papyrus:

Early gardens were laid out in formal, geometrical patterns. In cities, courtyards were favoured, which in Roman homes became 'outdoor rooms'. The walls enclosing these 'patios' were often painted with garden scenes to give an illusion of space.

> *I belong to you like this plot of land*
> *That I planted with flowers*
> *And sweet-smelling herbs.*
> *Sweet in its stream*
> *Shy by your hand*
> *Refreshing in the north wind.*
> *A lovely place to wander in*
> *Your hand in my hand.*

THE PURE LILY

Above all other flowers, the white or Madonna lily (*Lilium candidum*) is the symbol of purity. It is associated with the Virgin Mary, but its unsullied reputation goes back to the days of ancient Greece.

In Greek myth the lily sprang from the milk of Hera. In his desire to make his son Heracles, the child of a mortal woman, fully immortal, Zeus gave Hera a sleeping draught and put the child to her breast. He sucked so strongly the milk spurted out, creating the Milky Way. From drops that fell to earth lilies grew.

'Solomon in all his glory was not arrayed like one of these' is how Jesus refers to the 'lilies of the field' in the Sermon on the Mount.

A Spanish tale relates the fate of a poor boy, the son of a widow, who was unable to learn. Though sent by his mother to help the monks with their work, he could not even learn how to pray. He was eventually found dead in his cell, with a look of peace and joy on his face, and was buried in a quiet cemetery, his grave marked with a cross bearing the words, 'I believe in God; I hope for God; I love God.' Soon afterwards a white lily was seen flowering by the grave. When the tomb was opened the flower was discovered to be growing directly from his heart.

LILY LORE

- *Until it was picked by the Virgin, the lily was yellow, not white.*
- *The lily grew from Eve's tears when she was expelled from Paradise.*
- *In Christian iconography, the lily is carried by the angel Gabriel, who appeared to Mary at the Annunciation.*

SACRED FUNGI

Mushrooms (including toadstools and other fungi) are objects of fear and wonder. Because they spring up so quickly they were once thought to grow where lightning had struck.

Those who feared mushrooms thought them to be 'evil ferments of the earth'. The obvious reason for this is that many wild fungi are poisonous (a white mushroom was responsible for killing the Emperor Claudius). Among the ancient Hebrews, sacred mushrooms could be consumed only by the privileged, notably kings and priests. To all others they were taboo.

The Old Testament expression 'little foxes' is thought by some scholars to be code for mushroom juice that fortifies a man's sexual performance. This is echoed in a Russian name for chanterelles.

The mushroom Europeans held to be the sacred food of the gods was the fly agaric (*Amanita muscaria*) – a brilliant scarlet toadstool with white spots on its cap. The juice of this mushroom is believed to have been the 'ambrosia' of the Greek gods. The mushrooms were cooked and their juice was squeezed out between boards, then mixed with milk or curds. The same hallucinogenic liquid was revered by Hindus as a creation of Agni, god of mystic illumination and holy fire.

'One side will make you grow taller, and the other side will make you grow shorter.' That was how Lewis Carroll's caterpillar, sitting atop a fly agaric, explained to Alice the effects of mushroom eating. Her response on trying it was, 'Curiouser and curiouser.'

PLANT MUSIC

The hollow stems of plants were among the earliest musical instruments and, in graded sizes, combined to make the Pan pipes.

The god Pan, so the story goes, was in determined pursuit of the nymph Syrinx. Arriving at a river she cried out to the naiads there to save her – which they did, by turning her into reeds along the riverbank. Frustrated by his loss, Pan cut seven reeds and bound them together and so came to possess his love in spirit, if not in fact.

The flute was originally made of wood (and also of animal bone) and was known in China from the 9th century BC. The sound of this instrument is, many think, especially attractive to sheep and other animals, hence its long association with herdsmen. Like the Pan pipes, a flute makes a musical note when air blown into it vibrates inside the tube.

In New Guinea it is said that the flute was invented when a cassowary emerged with a buzzing sound from a slit in a bamboo cane a man was cutting. His wife was terrified at the noise and the man, thinking that he had discovered a sure way of frightening the opposite sex, ran to tell his friends of his find. With the aim of imitating the sound the bird had made, they fashioned the first ever bamboo flutes.

Hold a blade of grass tightly and vertically between your thumbs and blow against the thin edge. As the silica-packed blade vibrates you'll get a loud screech. Not exactly music, but another variation on the power of plants.

FRAGRANT SMOKE

One of the gifts brought by the Magi to the infant Jesus, frankincense, the 'sustenance of the gods', has long been burned to accompany and purify worship and was used in both East and West.

While they offered burnt resin to the sun god Ra at dawn, and myrrh at midday, the ancient Egyptians worshipped him with incense at sunset – in the fervent hope that he would return next morning. This evening incense, called *kyphi*, combined frankincense with other ingredients, including vanilla, cinnamon and mastic. While it was being mixed, readings were made from their sacred books.

The early Jews, who learned their practice from the Egyptians, used ceremonial incense made from 'four sweet scents', of which one was frankincense. It was also presented every Sabbath with the shewbread (the 12 unleavened loaves placed in the Tabernacle as an offering) and was stored, with other spices, in the great chamber of the House of God in Jerusalem.

The Old Testament tradition was later adopted by Christians and the use of incense, especially in a religious context (as well as for its healing properties) was firmly approved of by the Renaissance scholar and essayist Michel de Montaigne, who said of such scents: 'For myself [I] have often perceived that according to their strength and quality they change and alter and move my spirits, and work strong effects in me ...' He also praised the ability of incense '...to comfort, to quicken, to rouse, and to purify our senses so that we might appear apter and readier unto contemplations.'

MIND-CHANGING HEMP

Known since ancient times – and originally valued in practical terms for its flax-like fibres – hemp, the 'leaf of delusion' can have powerful effects on mood when burned or chewed.

Probably first harvested in China and northern India, hemp (*Cannabis sativa*) was described by the Greek historian Herodotus in the 5th century BC. Writing of the tribal customs of the Scythians, nomads who inhabited an area in what is now southern Russia, he wrote of how they 'take some of this hemp-seed, and, creeping under the felt coverings, throw it upon the red-hot stones; immediately it smokes, and gives out such a vapour as no Grecian vapour-bath can exceed; the Scyths, delighted, shout for joy ...'

What makes cannabis intoxicating is the resin in its leaves and seeds, which contains a whole spectrum of chemicals including cannabinoids. These act on the higher centres of the brain, producing an exhilarating feeling of intoxication, freedom from pain and even hallucinations.

From around 1000 BC bhang, a form of cannabis often mixed with milk to make a drink, was used in India as an anaesthetic and to treat all kinds of other ills. The ancient Greeks employed it as a remedy for earache.

A WEED BY ANY OTHER NAME
Street jargon for marijuana includes:

Devil drug – weed of madness – assassin of youth –
Mexican ditch weed – hashish – hay – chronic – blunts
– pot – brick weed – ganja – joint – Acapulco gold –
dime bag – rope – grass – weed – 'L' – jive stick –
nickel bag – MaryJane – loco – boom – indo – hydro
– green – skunk – puff – wacky baccy – grass – funk.

HEALTHY AND WISE

For almost every ailment you can name, whether of body or mind, there is a plant that will help effect a cure. Such is the depth and strength of herbal medicine. It is not hard to imagine how plants have earned their place as the sources of healing potions.

The evidence of such ancient healing exists both as the remains of seeds found in burial sites and in the records of early herbalists. As scientific notions of plant medicines developed, however, so too did the magical and mythical associations between plants and disease, so that it became commonplace to undertake rituals such as passing sick children through split ash trunks and eating garlic to keep away the ravages of vampires.

Animals – usually, but by no means always, dead ones – were widely used in ancient medicine. Often their application had more in common with sorcery than science, but the old-fashioned uses of leeches and maggots have regained a place in modern practice. It is understandable that some of the most bizarre remedies and prophylactics relate to the diseases that once mercilessly wiped out adults and children, including plague, whooping cough and tuberculosis, as well as mental illnesses and causes of unbearable pain such as toothache and gout.

Not all of nature's fauna and flora work for good. Bees and wasps sting (though bee stings are said to be able to cure rheumatism), while mosquitoes and fleas spread malaria and the plague and many plants contain poisons. Understanding the subtle difference between 'kill' and 'cure' is the legacy of science, which, embroidered with lore and legend, reveals fascinating stories.

WHAT'S IN A NAME?

Many plants with long-established healing properties have names – such as eyebright, heartsease and lungwort – that evocatively reflect the conditions they have traditionally been used to cure.

Eyebright (*Euphrasia officinalis*) gets its botanical name from the Greek word *euphraino*, 'to gladden', undoubtedly the result of its effective use in lotions and infusions to treat eye complaints. Often called euphrasy, its powers are extolled by Milton in *Paradise Lost*:

> *Michael from Adam's eyes the Film remov'd*
> *Which that false fruit that promis'd clearer sight*
> *Had bred; then purg'd with Euphrasie and Rue*
> *The visual Nerve, for he had much to see.*

The 'doctrine of signatures' dominated medical thought in the 16th and 17th centuries. It maintained that God had given us herbs to cure our ills, and as such they were appropriately marked. For example, the white-blotched leaves of lungwort (*Pulmonaria*), were thought to resemble lung tissue, and this was regarded as a sign that they could cure diseases of the lungs. Cultivated varieties have become well-loved garden plants.

Modern herbalists still recommend lungwort as a treatment for bronchitis, asthma, catarrh and other respiratory problems.

The effects of heartsease or pansy (most commonly *Viola tricolor*), the 'love-in-idleness' of romantic verse, may well be more emotional than physical. Traditionally symbolic of thoughts, it may be named from the French *pensée*, though Dr Johnson suggested that its name derived from 'panacea' – a cure for all ills.

In Shakespeare's A Midsummer Night's Dream, *heartsease yields its juice to jealous Oberon so that he can make Titania fall in love with 'some vile thing' – and she lights on Bottom the weaver.*

CHEWED FOR COMFORT

To ease the pain of indigestion, and the uncomfortable bloating that can accompany it, chewing on soothing seeds native to the Mediterranean and Western Asia is an old and effective remedy.

The seeds of fennel, dill and caraway – closely related plants – all contain natural oils that help soothe spasms in the intestine and calm flatulence. Caraway (*Carum carvi*), probably Europe's oldest cultivated spice, is used in Germany and the Netherlands to flavour cheese. Between the 16th and 19th centuries, caraway seed cake was baked to celebrate the end of the spring sowing of wheat.

Bitter fennel (*Foeniculum vulgare*), whose seeds taste rather like celery, was considered sacred by the Greeks. They believed that the Titan Prometheus had hidden fire in the hollow stalks of the fennel plant in order to steal it from the gods and bring it to humans.

> *Long favoured as a flavouring for pickled cucumbers and gherkins, dill* (Anethum graveolens) *gets its name from the Old Norse word* dilla, *to lull, because it was particularly used as an infusion for babies suffering from colic.*

CULPEPER'S RECOMMENDATIONS

The 17th-century herbalist Nicholas Culpeper endorsed the efficacy of these remedies:

- 'Carraway [sic] confits, once only dipped in sugar, and a half spoonful of them eating in the morning fasting, and as many after each meal, is a most admirable remedy, for those that are troubled with wind.'
- On fennel: '… the seeds, boiled in water, stays the hiccough, and takes way the loathings which oftentimes happen to the stomachs of sick and feverish persons …'
- 'The seed [of dill] is of more use than the leaves, and more effectual to digest raw and vicious humours. And is used in medicines that serve to expel wind, and the pains proceeding therefrom.'

ROOT CURES: GINGER AND LIQUORICE

Of all the plant roots that help a disturbed digestion, ginger and liquorice must rank among the most efficacious. Both these tropical plants are valued for both their flavour and their healing qualities.

Asia is the home of ginger (*Zingiber officinale*), which was described by the Greek physician Dioscorides, author of *De Materia Medica*, as being 'right good with meat in sauces … for it is of a heating and digesting qualitie, and is profitable for the stomacke'. It is the knobbly, swollen root or rhizome of ginger – which was one of the most prized imports of ancient Rome – that contains the pungent constituents that impart its characteristic flavour.

Liquorice tastes sweet because it contains glycyrrhizin, which is a substance 50 times sweeter than sucrose. The good news is that it is much less harmful to the teeth than sugar.

Liquorice (*Glycyrhizza glabra*), whose name means 'sweet root', was known to the Assyrians and Chinese. By 1305 it was so popular in England that Edward I taxed liquorice imports to raise money for the repair of London Bridge. The town of Pontefract, Yorkshire, is inextricably linked with liquorice. Here, in the 16th century, Dominican friars began cultivating the plant in quantity and making 'pomfrets' or pastilles of liquorice known as Pontefract cakes.

HEALING THE STOMACH

In the days before refrigeration, when digestive illnesses were rife, especially in warm countries, wearing an amulet to ward them off was common practice. Many of the motifs evoked the healing powers of animals and birds.

The ibis, often shown on an altar, and possibly tethered to papyrus reeds, was favoured as a talisman for healing ailments of the stomach. This bright red bird with its long, curved beak, sacred to the Egyptian god Thoth, was reputed to be able to devour serpents, reptiles and other harmful vermin. Greek amulets for the stomach were often heart-shaped or oval pieces of jasper, the grey-green mineral steatite or dark brown limonite, bearing inscriptions such as 'Good digestion' or 'Digest!'

Alexander of Tralles, the 6th-century Byzantine physician, confessed that for those patients who would not take the drugs he recommended or follow his prescribed health regime he was prepared to recommend amulets. For colic he recommended a stone engraved with 'Herakles standing upright and throttling a lion' set in a gold ring, which the patient would wear. The symbolism is clear – by invoking the strength of the hero the illness would be conquered.

To exert maximum effect, amulets were worn as close as possible to the troublesome area of the body.

The iconic image of a *chnoubis* – a thick-bodied snake with a lion's head encircled by projecting rays – was also thought to help improve digestive health, especially when it was carved into a piece of green jasper. This was thought to be effective by no less an authority than Galen, the Greek physician, who claimed to have tested it personally.

THE BETTER TO SEE YOU

Ancient tradition linked eye diseases and their cure with lizards and other reptiles. Though we rightly treat these ideas with suspicion, science has proved some old plant remedies to be effective.

In a magical procedure used by the Greeks, a green lizard would be blinded, then imprisoned in a new earthenware jar for nine days. Also put into the jar were ring stones carved with a lizard design. At the end of the

The gall of the green lizard was still, in the 13th century, commonly prescribed as a remedy for eye diseases. It is said that the giant lizard is blind because it chose from the gods the gift of poison in preference to sight.

nine days the lizard would have regained its sight, and would be freed. The stones, now imbued with healing 'magic', were used as amulets to cure eye diseases. For maximum effectiveness, the lizard's eyes needed to be put out with two iron pins, one in the left eye, the other in the right, and these pins used to set the stones into a ring.

In his *Natural History* Pliny talks of a small, wild cucumber whose 'seed is crushed and put in rain-water, where it sinks to the bottom. Then the action of the sun coagulates it, and this substance is made into tablet for the benefit of man. These are beneficial for the treatment of poor eyesight, eye diseases and styes on the lids.' Slices of cucumber are still popular for soothing the eyes, though these work simply because they are cool and moist.

Various purple fruits, including the bilberry and blackberry, have long reputations as being good for the eyesight. Both these fruits are now known to work by helping to improve the circulation in the smallest blood vessels.

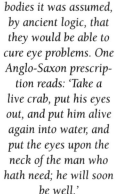

Crab cure: *Because crabs wear their eyes on stalks outside their bodies it was assumed, by ancient logic, that they would be able to cure eye problems. One Anglo-Saxon prescription reads: 'Take a live crab, put his eyes out, and put him alive again into water, and put the eyes upon the neck of the man who hath need; he will soon be well.'*

TREE CURES

Many trees have the reputation of being able to heal the sick. However, the records make clear that an accompanying ritual is considered necessary to make their remedies effective.

Most renowned for its healing powers is the ash tree. The 18th-century naturalist Gilbert White described in detail the ritual required for curing a sick child, though he was sceptical about the outcome. 'These [ash] trees, when young and flexible, were severed and held open by wedges, while ruptured children, stripped naked, were pushed through the apertures, under a persuasion that, by such a process, the poor babes would be cured of their infirmity.'

> *Cutting down an ash tree at a critical time according to the zodiac was an old way of curing a nosebleed.*

'As soon as the operation was over,' White continued, 'the tree, in the suffering part, was plastered with loam, and carefully swathed [bound] up. If the parts soldered and coalesced together, as usually fell out, where the feat was performed with any adroitness at all, the party was cured; but, where the cleft continued to gape, the operation, it was supposed, would prove ineffectual.'

In some places, washing the child in morning dew beforehand was considered an essential part of the procedure. In other localities children were passed nine times through the gap in the tree between the father and another man, the one saying, 'The Lord giveth,' and the other, 'The Lord receiveth.'

> *The aspen or 'shiver-tree' – the poplar whose branches shake in the wind – could, it was said, cure the ague if the sufferer pinned a lock of hair to a branch and said: 'Aspen-tree, aspen-tree, I prithee to shake and shiver instead of me.'*

HEALING BRANCHES

Make an offering to a tree – or sleep under it – and it may cure you. These are yet other ways in which people have sought to benefit from the powerful influence that trees exert.

Magical 'rag' trees, hung with strips of cloth which represented pleas for healing as well as other requests for improvements in fortune, were seen and recorded in Tunisia by Arnobius, an early Christian convert and denouncer of paganism, in the 4th century. In 1802 the French traveller Baron Dominique Vivant Denon (known as 'Napoleon's eye') also recorded such trees, bearing 'locks of hair, teeth, small leather pouches and little banners … The hair had been nailed there by women in order to fix their husbands' roving affections, and the teeth in supplication for a second set of teeth.'

Revering trees as places where angels or jinn descend, Arab people slept under them when sick, in the belief that they would receive a blessing in their dreams, which would restore their health.

At the Doon Well found in County Donegal, and in other places in Ireland, trees known as 'clooties' or 'raggety bushes', believed to have the spiritual power of healing, are still festooned with handkerchiefs, scarves and other items of clothing as well as rags and garlands of flowers. Their location near holy wells is linked to ancient belief in the healing powers of water. By the time the offering rots off the branch, the request for health will, it is said, have been granted. Another belief is that the tree itself bears the weight of the illnesses that people are trying to rid themselves of.

Rag trees are often hawthorns, trees associated with protection from the Evil Eye. Chopping one down is thought to bring bad luck.

TO CURE A FEVER

Fevers or agues, often the heralds of fatal diseases such as typhoid, smallpox and scarlet fever, were once rightly dreaded. No wonder, then, that 'animal magic' was widely used to cure them.

That a fever (or other illness) could be transferred to a passing animal was a common superstition. Cats – and dogs – were widely used for this purpose. Typically, an entry in *Notes & Queries* of 1892 relates: 'All my family being laid up with the influenza [we] … proposed to cut off some hair from the hollow of the neck, put it in milk, and give it to an animal to drink … The disease would then be transferred to the animal, and the patient would recover …' More drastic yet was a midwife's advice of 1888: 'If the baby is ill and not thriving, take a cat by the four feet, swing it round and round the infant several times then throw it out of the hole in the roof for letting out the smoke; if it is a black cat … then throw the cat out of the window; if the cat dies the child will live …'

> *Bizarre fever remedies include skinning a male mole, drying and powdering the pelt, then drinking it mixed with gin – or rubbing the soles of the feet with half a pigeon.*

> *Eating a live spider embedded in an apple, or in a spoonful of jam or treacle, is an old fever remedy. Hanging a 'necklace' of spiders around a fever patient until the animals died was a more drastic variation. Another was shutting a spider in a box until it expired.*

Passing a fevered child under an ass's belly three times was another way of bringing about a cure. This was most effective if the animal first ate some bread or a biscuit out of the child's lap.

THE DREADED COUGH

Whooping cough, now largely controlled by means of immunization, was once a fatal disease that families feared. The characteristic sound of the cough was often significant to the suggested cure.

As with fevers, the healing power of asses was commonly used to treat whooping cough, not least because of the similarity in sound of the animal's braying and the

noise made by the patient. Nine hairs taken from the white cross marking on a she-animal's back were hung in a bag around the child's neck. In some places children would be placed on asses' backs as soon as they were old enough, with the idea that this would protect them from catching the disease. And because of the luck associated with his mount, anyone riding a piebald horse was automatically consulted by those seeking a cure for the whooping cough.

Mistletoe was an old cure for whooping cough, with the bonus of bringing both good luck and freedom from attack by witches. For this reason it was left hanging in the house throughout the year, until a fresh bunch was brought in at Christmas to replace it.

Concoctions involving animals were widely recommended as whooping cough cures: mice could be roasted, fried, boiled in milk or baked in pies; owl soup and the slime of a snail mixed with sugar were witches' remedies. Plants were believed to be effective, too. Passing a child through a bramble arch – into which a plate of bread and butter was laid afterwards in a kind of ritual offering to evil spirits – was a common whooping cough treatment.

MORE CURES
According to old superstitions, you could cure whooping cough by:

- *Hanging a frog (because its croaking sounded like the cough) in the chimney.*
- *Putting a black beetle, a frog or a spider in a box and hanging it round the patient's neck. As the creature died, then decayed, so the illness would disappear.*
- *Drinking milk in which a live trout had been made to swim.*
- *Drinking from a cup made of ivy or holly wood.*

CALMING TONIC

'Folk medicine', though it may sometimes offer outlandish suggestions, has been the source of many genuine cures. Without it remedies for fever might well have remained elusive, gin would never have been mixed with tonic water, and willows would never have given us aspirin.

In 1638 the Countess of Chinchon, wife of the Governor of Peru, then a Spanish colony, was grievously ill with a fever. She was cured with the help of a local, native concoction prepared from the bark of a tree that now bears her name – the cinchona (*Cinchona officinalis*). Thanks to the fact that Jesuit missionaries spread word of its effectiveness, knowledge of the bark, discovered in 1820 to contain the substance quinine, became well known in Europe. This is why the cinchona is also dubbed the 'Jesuit tree'.

Mixing bitter quinine with lemon or lime to create a 'tonic water' to add to gin became a popular anti-malarial remedy and antidote to fever among British colonials in India. Granted a patent in 1858, it was introduced to the US by Schweppes only in 1953.

Edward Stone's interest in willow, which was known to the Greeks for its fever-reducing powers, arose from the doctrine of signatures, in which the nature of an illness provided the clue to its treatment. It was thus the propensity of fevers to occur in damp, watery places – where willows flourish – that set him on the right path.

Although effective, cinchona was expensive to import and it was this that drove Edward Stone, an Oxfordshire clergyman, to experiment with willow – another bitter bark – which led in due course to the discovery of aspirin. In 1763 he wrote to the Earl of Macclesfield, President of the Royal Society, describing how he had successfully treated patients suffering from fever (he called it ague) with 20 grains (about 1g) of powdered willow bark given every four hours in a dram (3.5ml) of water.

THE POPPY OF OBLIVION

The sleep-inducing effects of the opium poppy have made it the symbol of sleep, rest and peace. Because sleep can help to alleviate problems, this 'easer of all woes' is also a plant associated with consolation.

The opium poppy, with its large pink or white petals patched with purple at their base, has been hailed by poets for its soporific effect, as in the 19th-century 'Ode to Sleep' by Thomas Warton:

On this my pensive pillow, gentle sleep!
Descend, in all thy downy plumage drest;
Wipe with thy wing these eyes that wake
*   to weep,*
And place thy crown of poppies on my
*   breast.*

That the milky juice of the poppy is the source of a powerful drug was known in Neolithic times, and fields of poppies were grown along the Rhine in around 5000 BC. The ancient Greeks used opium extensively and the Roman naturalist Pliny, in the 1st century CE, wrote: 'A sleep-inducing drug is also obtained … by making incisions in the stalk when the buds are forming … Poppy juice is plentiful and becomes thick naturally and, fashioned into tablets, is dried in the shade.' Pliny was aware of the dangers of opium, admitting that 'if too much is swallowed, [it] brings about a fatal coma', and noting that it can also damage the eyesight.

By the 19th century, opium and its derivative, laudanum, were much used for pain relief, and addiction to this powerful narcotic often ensued. Thomas de Quincey, famously the author of Confessions of an English Opium Eater *(1822), declared it to be the centre of the true religion, of which he himself was the high priest.*

The sweet oblivion of death is marked by the red poppies that sprang so profusely from Flanders fields in World War I. The poppy is now used symbolically by the Royal British Legion to remember all those who have fallen in war.

HERBS FOR A BETTER NIGHT'S SLEEP

Valerian, lavender, hops and many other herbs are well known for their power to help us nod off, and chamomile tea is the best nightcap.

Valerian (*Valeriana officinalis*) was recommended as a remedy for insomnia by the Greek physician Galen. It became popular in Europe in the 16th century and is now known to work on the brain like a very mild version of Valium and similar tranquillizers.

The cone-like fruits of hops (*Humulus lupulus*), as well as flavouring beer, are traditionally dried and used to make 'hop pillows', with a smell redolent of musty apples. When, in his 'madness', King George III was having trouble sleeping, it was a hop pillow that helped to solve his problem. Lavender (*Lavandula*) is another soothing herb, described as a 'comfort to the brain' by the 16th-century English herbalist William Turner.

> *The calming juice of lettuce* (Lactuca sativa), *has earned its place in literature in the opening lines of Beatrix Potter's* The Tale of the Flopsy Bunnies: *'It is said that the effect of eating too much lettuce is "soporific". I have never felt sleepy after eating lettuces; but then I am not a rabbit.'*

MORE HELP FOR THE WAKEFUL

Some other sleep-inducing folk remedies include:

- *Lemon (bee) balm* (Melissa officinalis) – *native to the Eastern Mediterranean and once also used as a charm to drive away evil spirits.*
- *A goat's horn put under the head.*
- *The left eye of a hedgehog, fried in oil.*
- *Catnip* (Nepeta cataria) – *intoxicating to cats and helpful to human insomniacs.*

THE LIVING PHARMACY

Remains in ancient burial sites over 60,000 years old show how long humans have been using plants to heal their ills. While many modern drugs have been synthesized to mimic the actions of plants, herbal remedies are still respected.

To disguise an often bitter taste, the Egyptians mixed their herbal remedies with honey, and even buried their dead with supplies of opium to keep them comfortable in the afterlife.

Marsh mallow for sore throats and intestinal upsets and grape hyacinth to encourage urination are among the earliest of all known natural remedies, believed to have been used by Neanderthals living in the 'fertile crescent', now part of Iraq. And ephedra, still valued for treating asthma, was one of more than 250 plants recorded in the most ancient Chinese herbal, the *Pen Tsao Ching*, said to date from around 3000 BC. Herbal medicine was greatly developed by the Egyptians, who discovered simple ways to extract the useful ingredients that plants contain, and by the Greeks and Romans.

The 'physick' gardens of medieval monks were devoted to the cultivation of medicinal plants, but country folk also drew on native plants for countless other remedies. Particularly favoured were 'cure-alls', plants such as betony, employed against everything from hangovers to nosebleeds, and vervain, the 'divine weed', which as well as curing plague and healing the bites of rabid dogs could even deflect the forces of sorcery and witchcraft.

'It shall be lawful to every person ... having Knowledge and Experience of the Nature of Herbs, Roots and Waters ... to practise, use and minister in and to any outward Sore, Uncome wound, Apostumations, outward Swelling or Disease ... according to their Cunning, Experience and Knowledge in any of the Diseases, Sores and Maladies beforesaid ... without suit, vexation, trouble, penalty, or loss of their goods.'

(Charter of Rights for Herbalists, 1543)

FULL OF (COFFEE) BEANS

Once dubbed 'the Devil's drink', coffee has its good and bad sides as far as health is concerned. For some it has even led to the making of fortunes.

A sheep herder in Kaffa, Ethiopia, is said, in Arab legend, to have made a drink from the red 'cherries' of a strange-looking shrub and, as a result, found himself extraordinarily wakeful. Another story of the period, sometime before 1000 CE, relates how an Arab was banished to the desert to die but survived by boiling and eating the fruits of an unknown plant. The drink was called Mocha after the nearest town, whose inhabitants viewed the outcast's survival as an omen.

In the late 16th century, Pope Clement VIII made coffee acceptable to Christians (and no longer a drink of infidels) by 'baptizing' it.

Thus were the stimulating powers of caffeine first experienced, but it was not until the 17th century that coffee drinking became common in the West, and the coffee houses became fashionable meeting places. It was one such house, opened by Edward Lloyd in 1688 and frequented by ships' captains, merchants and ship owners, that was the origin of Lloyd's of London, which became the world's most famous insurance market.

The 19th-century housewife was recommended to use roasted coffee to rid a house of noxious smells, including those made by 'animal and vegetable effluvia'.

Sir Henry Salter, an eminent Victorian doctor, recommended strong black coffee as a treatment for asthma. And it has now been confirmed that caffeine is a chemical cousin of modern asthma medicines (xanthines). It has also been proved to boost brainpower, increase stamina during exercise, increase sperm count and even lower the risks of colon cancer and diabetes. On the downside, anyone with sleep problems needs to avoid coffee. Indeed, one name the early Arab traders gave it was *qahwa*, which means 'that which prevents sleep'. Heart palpitations, raised blood pressure and heightened anxiety are other problems caffeine can aggravate.

TEA: THE CUP THAT HEALS

Whether you drink it green, black or with milk, tea is the beverage that really does you good. Though the infamous Boston Tea Party sparked a war, a get-together for 'a nice cup of tea' is great for the spirits.

Though tea (botanically *Camellia sinensis*) was introduced to Europe from China in the 16th century, it took another 200 years for it to become affordable by the masses. The feel-good effects of tea have long been known – and William Gladstone described them in 1865: 'If you are cold, tea will warm you; if you are too heated it will cool you; if you are depressed, it will cheer you; if you are excited it will calm you.'

Earl Grey tea was named for Charles Grey, 2nd Earl Grey. It is said that he was given the recipe, which includes oil of bergamot, by a Chinese mandarin whose son's life he had saved.

A happy accident: *One day in 2737 BC, as the legendary Chinese emperor Shen-nung's servant boiled his master some water for a drink, a leaf from a nearby bush blew into it. The emperor decided to taste the brew. So runs the legend of tea's 'discovery', but tea drinking was not fully documented until the 8th century, when* Ch'a Ching, *a comprehensive manual by Lu Yu, was published.*

The medical evidence has been mounting ever since. Green tea is especially rich in antioxidants, whose role in the body is to mop up the free radicals that can harm the heart and may trigger cancer. Antioxidants may also lower levels of harmful cholesterol. And there is just enough caffeine in tea to perk you up and keep you alert without giving you the shakes.

FOXGLOVE TO STRENGTHEN THE HEART

With its tall stems and conical purplish flowers, the foxglove (*Digitalis* sp) is not only one of the most attractive wildflowers but, medicinally, one of the most potent. As well as stimulating the heart it has also been used to ease pain and calm fevers.

It was probably the ancient Egyptians who, around 300 BC, first made use of the fact that the foxglove, though poisonous, has the power to strengthen and improve the heartbeat. But the plant's true potential was only realized in the 18th century thanks to an English doctor, William Withering, who started looking for a cure for dropsy, a state of severe water retention (now known as oedema), which may be caused by congestive heart failure.

It was Withering's luck, in around 1775, to encounter a folk remedy which, although it made patients vomit, also made the dropsy symptoms disappear. After much experimentation he came to the conclusion that a constituent of dried foxglove leaves (now identified as digitalin) would improve the heartbeat and extend a fading lifespan.

FOXGLOVE TRADITIONS

There are many other stories featuring the foxglove:

- The fairies give the blooms to foxes to put over their paws and prevent them being heard when they raid chicken coops at night.
- Because a strong poison lurks in its attractive flowers the foxglove is a symbol of insincerity.
- If anyone hears a foxglove bell ring, death is imminent.
- The bells of a foxglove ring to warn foxes that hunters are approaching.
- Foxgloves will heal skin sores, but only if gathered from the north side of a hedge.

THE BLESSED GARLIC BULB

It is said that to stay healthy you should never go a day without garlic. Quite apart from its reputation for keeping vampires at bay, garlic is truly a medical wonder.

The disadvantage of garlic is its effect on the breath. There are lots of ways to neutralize its sulphurous odours, including chewing parsley, apple, aniseed or liquorice. But, as it's said in parts of France: 'If everybody ate garlic then no one would find it objectionable.'

Is there anything that garlic can't help? Certainly it is one of the most effective plants in preventing everything from infections to cancer – and for treating problems with circulation, digestion and respiration, including coughs and colds. It contains allicin, a sulphur compound, and a range of antiseptic and anti-inflammatory phenols and flavonoids, which have been proved to be able to prevent the formation and growth of cancer cells.

The Egyptians were the first to fully appreciate its powers. They hung strings of it around children's necks to get rid of worms, and workmen constructing the Great Pyramid were given a daily ration by the pharaoh Khufu to endow them with strength and prevent them falling ill.

MORE GARLIC TALES

- *Believing it would give them courage, Roman soldiers ate garlic before battle.*
- *From the use of garlic to cure their condition, or perhaps in an unkind reference to their bald heads looking like peeled garlic, lepers were called 'pilgarlics'.*
- *During World War I, when first aid supplies were in short supply, garlic was used as an antiseptic.*
- *In the Middle Ages, garlic was much eaten by heavy drinkers, in the belief that it would prevent drunkenness.*

ST JOHN'S WORT PICK-ME-UP

It is apt that the demons of depression should be put to flight by St John's wort, the herb once given to the possessed and now proven to contain chemicals that lift the mood. Fragrant lavender flowers, infused in boiling water, are another tried and tested means of relieving mental gloom.

Once known as the 'fairy herb', St John's wort (*Hypericum perforatum*) was revered by the Greeks for its power to ward off evil spirits. In Christian times, pieces of the plant, picked the previous morning, were hung over doors on St John's day, 24 June, to purify homes. The powers of the plant (traditionally it was also used as an application to speed the healing of wounds) were associated with the fact that, when burnt, it exuded an aroma like incense – itself a purifier – the 'perfume reserved for God' (see page 101).

Centuries before lavender (*Lavandula*) was used to make scented bags to perfume closets, the Romans sprinkled lavender flowers in their bath water. 'Swimming of the braine' was one of the many conditions John Gerard treated with the herb. An old way of administering lavender was to put sprigs of the plant into a cap to wear on the head.

> *The lavender got its scent, it's said, when the Virgin Mary spread the clothes of the infant Jesus on the bushes to dry.*

BLOOD-LETTING LEECHES

The idea of curing patients by letting leeches suck their blood began in Egypt some 2500 years ago. The practice has now been revived to help prevent blood clotting immediately following surgery.

Bloodletting by leeches, thought to be able to cure everything from obesity and laryngitis to mental illness, reached its height in the 1800s. The Victorian self-help manual *Enquire Within* equipped its readers with the practical knowledge to use leeches for themselves. It advised shaving the skin before the leech was applied, adding the reassurance that 'if the leech is hungry it will soon bite'. In case of adherence problems it suggested one should '… roll the leech into a little porter [ale], or moisten the surface with a little blood, or milk, or sugar, or water'. If leeches were to be applied to the gums it warned that a 'leech glass' should be used to keep them in place, otherwise they 'are apt to creep down the patient's throat'.

Bloodletting by leeches was thought to restore the balance of the four humours – blood, phlegm, black bile and yellow bile – on which Western medicine was based from the time of the ancient Greeks until as late as the 19th century.

The use of leeches declined in the 19th century, but surgeons are again making use of the creature's remarkable physiology today. As it sucks blood it not only produces an anticoagulant, which prevents clotting, but also a mild anaesthetic, which makes its actions painless. What's more, the leech's gut is home to a bacterium that not only aids the digestion of blood but produces an antibiotic that helps prevent secondary infection.

The word 'leech' comes from the Old English laece, *which is related to* lacnian, *'to heal'. At one time it was applied not only to the bloodsucking annelids but also to the doctors who prescribed their use.*

TO DRIVE OUT ILLNESS

All manner of animal products were used in the past to dispel disease. And to keep evil witches at bay – and give protection against the illnesses they

**caused to humans and livestock – animal parts were
sealed inside glass bottles and buried.**

Fat, flesh and blood, as well as the ground hoofs and
horns of animals and birds – including
the ox, ass, goat, deer, lion, mouse, bat,
frog, lizard, snake, swallow, duck and
goose – were common 'medicines' in the
Egyptian armoury against disease. Many
of these are mentioned specifically in the
Ebers papyrus, which dates from around
1500 BC, and is the oldest preserved
medical document in existence.

*The ancients believed
greatly in the process
of fumigation in
driving out the demons
that caused disease.
Animal parts would be
swallowed or the body
smeared with mixtures
such as the dung of a
swallow or goose mixed
with the hair of an ass.*

The aim of the 'witch bottle' was to
lure the disease or other harm aimed
at you into the bottle, where it could
be safely confined. To be most effective
it needed to contain material from the
person or animal thought to be under threat. This could
be blood, hair, nail parings or urine. One such bottle,
containing mostly cow fat, was unearthed in Dorset in
2005. It is thought to date from the mid-1700s, when
outbreaks of cattle distemper are known to have ram-
paged through local herds.

EGYPTIAN CURES

*Some bizarre animal medicines and treatments
detailed in ancient papyri include:*

To drive out illness from the tongue
– *goose fat.*

To ease stiffness in a limb – *hippo
fat, or the fat of a silurus fish.*

**To prevent lashes growing on the
eyelids after they have been pulled
out** – *blood of a pig, dog or oryx.*

To cure women's problems –
*'fumigate her eyes with the legs of
the bee-eater … then make her eat
the liver of an ass, raw.'*

To cure earache – *syringe the ears
with the gall of a bull, goat or
sheep.*

MAGGOT CLINIC

Eating away illness – literally – is the medical role of the maggot, in an old technique now coming back into use. But maggots need to be carefully chosen and handled to prevent them causing more problems than they cure.

Maggots have been known for their healing powers since the 16th century, but maggot therapy began in earnest following the American Civil War and World War I, when battlefield medics noticed that soldiers' wounds that were infested with maggots healed better than those where no maggots were present.

The larvae of blowflies, maggots are now used to treat ulcers and other 'flesh-eating' conditions to prevent them become gangrenous. Such treatment is particularly useful for patients who are allergic or resistant to antibiotics.

Though pain-free, maggot treatment does not look pleasant, and it can also cause almost unbearable tickling.

Fantastical verses: It was an old belief that eccentric or crotchety people had maggots in their brains, which is why 'maggoty' is another word for 'whimsical'. In this vein, Samuel Wesley, father of Charles and John, wrote Maggots: Or, Poems On Several Subjects, Never Before Handled. *The titles of these eccentric verses included 'The Bear Fac'd Lady', 'To My Gingerbread Mistress', 'A Dialogue, Between Chamber-pot and Frying Pan' and 'A Pindarique on the Grunting of a Hog'.*

As the maggots devour the infected tissue they clean the skin, preventing the growth of potentially fatal infection. Once the maggots have done their job – by which time they may have increased up to ten times in size – the doctor simply flushes them out.

JUST A FLEA BITE?

Proverbially something hardly worth bothering with, flea bites can certainly be irritating. And we are lucky that fleas no longer carry the dreaded plague.

Between 1348 and 1357 the bubonic plague, known as the Black Death, wiped out at least a quarter of the population of Europe. 'It is impossible to believe the number who have died,' wrote a French monk, adding: 'Travellers, merchants, pilgrims declare that they have found cattle wandering without herdsmen in fields, towns and wastelands.'

The parasitical lifestyle of fleas is celebrated in rhyme: 'Great fleas have little fleas/Upon their backs to bite 'em/Little fleas have lesser fleas/And so ad infinitum.'

The plague was not a new disease, having certainly struck the Athenians in 430 BC, during the Peloponnesian War, but what neither the ancients nor the medieval citizens knew was that this dread contagion was spread by the bites of fleas, which had, in turn, feasted on the blood of infected black rats. Fleas also carry typhus, another potentially deadly disease.

OUT, DREAD FLEAS
Some flea legends and remedies from around the world:

- *Air your beds before Easter and fleas will not trouble you all summer. (English)*
- *Fleas were created to make work for women. (Flemish)*
- *God sent the flea to earth to punish humans for their laziness. (Danish)*
- *Put splinters from a tree struck by lightning in a house to drive out fleas. (American)*
- *If a flea bites you on the hand it is good luck – it will not bother you again. (German)*
- *On 1 March, clean the house and smash an earthenware pot against the door while you cry: 'Out with fleas and mice.' (Greek)*

MOSQUITOES – THE FLYING FOE

As notorious as the flea for its ability to spread disease, the mosquito is a potentially deadly pest when it passes on malaria or yellow fever. These two diseases have, between them, killed more people than all the wars in history.

The Mosquito Coast or Mosquitia region lies on the east coast of Nicaragua and Honduras. The name, used by Paul Theroux for his 1981 novel, is derived from the Miskito, the indigenous inhabitants. The hordes of biting insects found in their territory were reputedly able to kill a man in a single night.

It is the female mosquito that packs the fatal punch. As she punctures human skin with her long proboscis she may inject, at the same time, the larval forms of a parasite or a virulent virus. The pairings are specific. The malaria parasite *Plasmodium* is carried by the *Anopheles* mosquito, the yellow fever virus by *Aedes aegypti*. Evening is the time when humans are most vulnerable to attack, because, as one medical wit has put it, the mosquito, like other sinners, 'prefers the night hours for its revels'.

The way to stop a mosquito biting you is, it's said, to hold your breath when the insect alights on you. More practical methods include driving them away with clouds of smoke from a fire or protecting oneself with a mosquito net – or destroying the habitats where they breed. Among the places where the latter has been achieved are the notorious lands astride the Panama Canal. During Ferdinand de Lesseps' attempt to create this waterway in the 1880s thousands of workers died from malaria and yellow fever, causing the French diplomat and engineer to abandon his dream. The swamps were drained and filled, and the canal was eventually completed by the USA.

PLANT PURGES – NASTY MEDICINE

Of all the medicines once forced by parents on to their reluctant children, old-fashioned cures for constipation were among the nastiest. A 'spoonful of sugar' was most certainly needed to help these medicines go down.

'Being regular', while still regarded as important to health, is no longer the obsession it once was. So much so that anyone prone to constipation would be dosed with everything from mild laxatives to violent purges. Many of the remedies came from plants, but not the natural fibre in vegetables, fruit and cereals. Instead, castor oil, senna and other foul medicines were given, often daily.

Castor oil, extracted from the seeds of the plant *Ricinus communis*, was the Victorians' favourite constipation remedy.

In World War I soldiers suffering from constipation took to drinking the castor oil used to lubricate early aeroplane engines to ease their discomfort – often with drastic effects.

The Egyptians valued castor oil as fuel for their lamps. It was so important that seeds were buried in tombs to equip the departed for their future life.

Long before this Dioscorides, the Greek pharmacologist, declared that although valuable as a purgative it was 'not fit for food'. He was certainly right, in that the seeds, if eaten whole, can quickly kill, since they contain lethal toxins.

The laxative effect of senna (*Cassia angustifolia*), which was probably discovered by Arab physicians in the 10th century, resides in the chemicals contained in its seeds and pods. Because it is 'apt to gripe' when given alone, senna was traditionally mixed with ginger, cloves, cinnamon or nutmeg to mollify its effects and improve its taste.

HEALING ESSENCES

Using highly scented plant essences to heal and relax body and mind is an ancient practice now known as aromatherapy. The key to the treatment lies in the essential oils that many plants produce in glands located in their leaves, petals, stems or bark.

In his praise of aromatic plants, Hippocrates, the Greek 'father of medicine', is reported to have declared that the way to health is to have an aromatic bath and a scented massage every day.

The history of aromatherapy has no exact beginning, but the Chinese certainly valued plant oils, and burned incense to create feelings of well-being. This and other herbal preparations, including distilled cedarwood oil, were much used by the Egyptians, both for improving the health and fragrance of the living and for embalming the dead. Their knowledge passed to the Greeks and Romans.

Distillation was used by the Persians to make fragrant flower waters from roses and orange blossoms. The technique was improved in the 11th century, when the Persian physician and philosopher Avicenna invented a coiled pipe that was able to produce more concentrated oils. Although herbal preparations were widely used from medieval times, real interest in essential oils revived only when the French chemist, René Gattefosse, having burned himself badly, plunged his hand into a container of lavender oil. The wound healed and left no scar, an outcome that encouraged him to use similar treatments on soldiers injured in World War I.

SOME ESSENTIAL OILS AND THEIR BENEFITS

Cedarwood – *sedative; good for anxiety, coughs and bronchitis.*

Rose – *relaxing, soothing; helps to lift depression and clear headaches.*

Tea tree – *antiseptic, cleansing; best for thrush, insect bites, spots, sores and other skin conditions.*

Lemon – *refreshing, stimulating; can help to improve circulation and lower blood pressure.*

Hyssop – *decongestant; helps breathing problems.*

Fennel – *soothes the gut; eases indigestion.*

Juniper – *relaxing and refreshing; good for arthritis and insomnia.*

EFFICACIOUS CHAMOMILE

Chamomile, arguably the most versatile of healing herbs, comes in two varieties, German and Roman, both highly regarded for their therapeutic effects.

Because fresh chamomile has a distinct apple aroma, which gives no hint of its bitter taste, the Greeks called it 'ground apple'. Its fragrance is released when crushed, so it was strewn on medieval floors as a room freshener and was often planted in green walks in gardens. Indeed, tramping over the plant seems especially beneficial to its reproduction, as the old rhyme claims:

In addition to its many therapeutic uses, chamomile enhances the fairness of blonde hair.

Like a chamomile bed –
The more it is trodden
The more it will spread.

The Greeks regarded chamomile with respect, prescribing it for fevers and agues as well as menstrual and other female problems. English herbalists also swore by its healing effects. By the 17th century, Nicholas Culpeper was able to produce a long list of its 'virtues', saying that: 'It moderately comforts all parts that have need of warmth, digests and dissolves whatsoever has need thereof, by a wonderful speedy property.'

William Turner, the 16th-century English physician and divine, was effusive in his praise of chamomile, especially used after bathing. He said (using modern spelling): 'It hath flowers wonderfully shining yellow and resembling the apple of an eye … It will restore a man to his colour shortly if a man after the long use of the bath drink of it after he is come forth out of the bath. … This herb was consecrated by the wise men of Egypt unto the Sun and was reckoned to be the only remedy of all agues.'

THE SOVEREIGN REMEDY
Just some of the many conditions believed over the ages to be helped by chamomile:

Aches and pains – anxiety – asthma – bacterial infections – colic – conjunctivitis – cramp – depression – digestive disorders – eczema – fatigue – fever – flatulence – gout – haemorrhoids – herpes – influenza – insomnia – jaundice – laryngitis – menstrual pain – migraine – mouth infections – nappy rash – neuralgia – pruritis – rheumatism – sprains – skin infections – sinusitis – swelling – ulcers – viral infections.

CURING EAR PROBLEMS

Before the advent of antibiotics and other modern medicines, earaches and temporary deafness were not only painful but hard to cure. All kinds of treatments were tried, though the literature is typically vague as to their effectiveness.

Old 'natural' remedies for earache were rich and varied, from rinsing the ears with warm onion juice or the sap of a pine tree to syringing with the gall of a bull or goat – also warmed. One of the Oxyrhynchus Papyri (a collection of manuscripts salvaged from an ancient garbage heap in Egypt and containing writings by classical Greek authors) instructs that one should 'Thoroughly moisten a flock of wool with the gall of an ox, roll up and insert.'

The earwig or 'ear beetle' gets its name from the old but erroneous belief that it could not only enter the ear but penetrate the brain, causing serious damage.

Olive oil is another remedy for earache, while herbalists recommend mixing it with Aaron's rod, the great mullein (*Verbascum thapsus*). In both Europe and Asia this plant was credited with the power to drive away evil spirits and protect against black magic.

An old Romany remedy for temporary deafness caused by the build-up of wax involved the use of the fat of the 'hotchi-witchi' or hedgehog. 'Melt the fat and pour a drop into the ear at night,' it recommended, adding, 'A good substitute for the hedgehog fat is the fat of the ordinary goose.' Treatment of one ear at a time, on alternate nights, was deemed most effective.

EASING THE TOOTHACHE

Until you can get to the dentist, natural medicines may help relieve the pain of toothache. Luckily our prospects for a quick, permanent cure are hugely

better than they were for our forebears, who would stop at almost nothing to relieve the pain.

Grandma's favourite remedy for toothache was oil of cloves – or gently chewing a clove. Cloves are the dried flower buds of the clove tree (*Syzygium aromaticum*), and contain the substance eugenol, which is both anaesthetic and antiseptic. Another country treatment is the richly fragrant meadowsweet (*Filipendula ulmaria*), now known to be rich in chemicals closely related to aspirin.

Though it was probably named for the tooth-like scales on its roots, the parasitic toothwort (Lathraea squamaria), which grows on the roots of alder, elm and hazel, is an old-fashioned remedy for toothache.

Before decayed and painful teeth could be preserved with fillings, extraction was the only cure. In preference to forcible and excruciating tooth removal, Pliny recommended the berry of the 'large juniper', which, he said, 'breaks the teeth and makes them fall out, thus relieving the pain'. His even more fanciful recommendation was to use an iron tool to draw a line around an erigeron (fleabane) plant, pull it up, then touch the offending tooth with the plant three times. The plant should then be replanted 'in its original spot so as to keep it alive, [so that] … the tooth will never ache again'.

A paw cut from a mole – preferably a live one – is an old cure for toothache. Pliny recommended another equally cruel treatment: 'At full moon cut off the head of a swallow that has been fed in the morning, tie it in linen and hang it up.'

AGAINST THE GOUT

Gout is such an excruciatingly painful condition that sufferers would once try any plausible remedy to relive their symptoms – even the consumption of dried bats.

All kinds of herbal mixtures have traditionally been used against the gout, an ailment caused by crystals of uric acid, which collect in the joints, with the big toe usually the first to be afflicted. The name comes from the old French *goute*, meaning 'drop'. This is because it was thought to be caused by 'drops of humours'.

It's no myth that cherries are good for gout. It has been proved that eating about 8oz (225g) of cherries a day really can lower the levels of uric acid in the blood.

A German doctor, Adrian Mynsicht, famous in the 17th century, invented an 'elixir of vitriol' containing cinnamon, ginger, cloves, nutmeg, sage, mint, cubebs (a pungent pepper), aloes, lemon peel, calamus aromaticus (sweet sedge), galangal root (a relative of ginger) and sugar. In England, a century later, the preferred remedy was the Duke of Portland's powder, so named because the Duke had been cured by it at a Swiss resort. It had been a favourite in Italy for centuries, and contained gentian root, germander, birthwort and centaury.

Pliny maintained that bathing the legs with water in which a fox had been boiled would ease the gout.

Folk remedies include the right foot of a frog wrapped in deerskin or a 'mummified' owl, plucked and baked slowly in the oven, then pounded to a powder and mixed with boar fat and raven broth.

A ROMANY RECIPE
To treat the gout:

1oz (25g) woundwort
1oz (25g) powdered rhubarb root
1oz (25g) willow bark
Boil together in 3 pints (1.5 litres) water for 15 minutes.
Strain. Take two tablespoonfuls night and morning.

HAIR TOMORROW?

All manner of natural remedies have been suggested as cures for baldness, though none takes account of the inevitability of hair loss whose cause is genetic.

Bear grease and maidenhair (a type of fern) mixed with 'ladanum' was, declared Pliny, a way to prevent baldness, as long as it was mixed with 'lamp-black from lamp-wicks and the soot that collects in the curved nozzles'.

Rosemary features in restorative recipes old and new. One 1920s remedy suggested rubbing the hair for about a quarter of an hour with a mixture of rosemary, paraffin oil, white wax, rum, castor oil and beef marrow. Spirits of rosemary plus oil of sesame, oil of lemon, strong liquor of ammonia and chloroform was another remedy: it risked rendering the 'patient' quite senseless, whatever it did to their hair.

Based on the scientific fact that it prevents the formation, from the male hormone testosterone, of a substance known to kill off the hair follicles, saw palmetto is a herb recommended to slow down hair loss, even if it only puts off the inevitable. For men prone to prostate problems, the added advantage of saw palmetto berries is that they promote urine flow.

PAIN FROM PLANTS

Stinging nettles and – in North America – poison ivy are the most damaging plants that most of us are likely to encounter when out and about. In both cases, it is possible that other plants growing nearby may provide at least temporary relief from the symptoms they provoke.

The nettle (*Urtica dioica*) delivers its stings in hairs which, when they break off in the skin, inject tiny shots of inflammation-causing histamine. In Irish mythology, however, they are said to be the prongs of the Devil's pitchfork. Putting a leaf of the dock (*Rumex*) on the sting can give some immediate cooling relief from the pain, but severe stings may need antihistamine treatment.

> *Nettle rash is a generic term for an itchy, allergy-provoked eruption on the skin that looks similar to nettle stings. An old cure for it is nettles themselves, boiled up and made into a tea.*

Poison ivy, the climber *Rhus toxicodendron*, does its worst by producing an irritant oil called urushiol, which, when it touches the skin, causes a persistent blistering rash (though some lucky people are immune to its effects). How to identify it? 'Leaves of three, let them be; Berries white, run in fright' is the old rhyme. Even looking at it, especially in wet, foggy, weather, is said to bring on an attack. To protect themselves the Cherokee are known to address the plant as 'My friend' and, if poisoned rub the affected part with crawfish flesh. Of proven plant antidotes, the most renowned is the juice of the succulent jewelweed (*Impatiens capensis*).

IN PRAISE OF NETTLES

Stinging nettles have their good points, not least through their inclusion in many old remedies, such as:

- For baldness: 'Dip the teeth of your comb every morning in the expressed juice of nettles, and comb the hair the wrong way. It will surprisingly quicken its growth.' (Medieval tip)
- Deliberate stinging with nettles warms the body and guards against cold. (Ancient Roman treatment, employed in cold climates)
- When baked with sugar, nettles make 'the vital spirits more fresh and lively'. (John Gerard, 16th century)

DEADLY VEGETATION

Plants notorious for their toxicity include deadly nightshade, laburnum and monkshood. Mistaken identity is a recurring reason for tragic accidents with deadly vegetation.

Documenting plant poisoning in the Victorian era, Alfred Taylor, a lecturer in jurisprudence, recorded many cases in great detail. Two involving monkshood (*Aconitum napellus*) were typical. 'In 1842,' he recounts, 'a lady residing in Lambeth was poisoned by her having eaten the root in mistake for horseradish with some roast beef ... she died in three hours.' Also, 'A boy similarly died after using the leaves "for parsley".' All parts of this plant, also called wolfbane, are poisonous. The Greeks believed it sprang up at the entrance to Hades, where the saliva of the hell-dog Cerberus had dripped.

> *What many poisonous plants have in common is their bitter taste. This gives us a kind of protection, for of all the taste buds on our tongues those that respond to bitterness are by far the most sensitve.*

In another of Taylor's accounts, the poisoning was deliberate. In Inverness in 1843 '... a youth, with the intention of merely producing vomiting in one of his fellow-servants, a female, put some dry laburnum bark into the broth which was being prepared for their dinner. The cook, who remarked "a strong peculiar taste" in the broth, soon became very ill.' She did recover, though this took over a year, but laburnum is renowned for cases of poisoning, especially when the seeds, in bean-like pods, are eaten by children, who pick them up in the garden.

> *Of all the poisonous plants in the flora hemlock (Conium maculatum) has one of the most virulent reputations. This potent relative of parsley was used in ancient times as a bona fide medicine. The many conditions treated with sparing doses of hemlock include rheumatism, ulcers, neuralgia, tetanus and syphilis. Culpeper recommended laying hemlock leaves on the brow to soothe inflamed eyes.*

Nux vomica – *packed with the deadly alkaloid strychnine, which can have cumulative effects, hence its use in cases of deliberate poisoning.*

Henbane (Hyoscamus niger) – *contains the narcotic hyoscine, which kills by causing delirium, loss of speech and paralysis.*

Deadly nightshade (Atropa belladonna) – *the source of the sedative atropine, which dilates the pupils (hence its name, meaning 'beautiful lady'); it is said to be the 'insane root' mentioned in Shakespeare's* Macbeth.

Thornapple, madapple or Devil's apple (Datura stramonium) – *contains a strong narcotic whose effects are similar to those of henbane. The fresh leaves, when bruised, emit a foetid odour.*

TO HEAL A WOUND

Though the body has remarkable powers of self-healing, assistance is sometimes necessary to stitch a gash, prevent infection and speed repair – in all of which animals and plants have roles to play.

Possibly because they were thought to be lucky, spiders' webs have been used to dress wounds since the 1st century CE. And 1500 years later, Shakespeare has Bottom say, in *A Midsummer Night's Dream*, 'I shall desire you of more acquaintance, good master Cobweb. If I cut my finger, I shall make bold of you.' What the cobweb does, think modern scientists, is protect against infection thanks to the chemical coating on the silk. (This is also helpful to the spider, stopping webs from being rotted away by bacteria and fungi.)

Named for its powers: comfrey (Symphytum officinale) *lives up to its common names (which include knitbone, knitback, gum plant and consolida) because it contains allantoin, a substance that promotes tissue regeneration.*

Honey, once eaten by Greek athletes to improve their performances, is, as the Romans knew, a perfect dressing for wounds that need to be kept clean. Modern practice bears out the sense behind this ancient remedy, though why honey should kill bacteria – as well as reducing inflammation and scarring – remains a mystery. Equally elusive is the reason why honey from bees that feed on the manuka bush (*Leptospermum scoparium*), a wild Antipodean relative of the myrtle, should be most effective.

Sprinkling a wound with cayenne or black pepper is an old way of stopping bleeding in an emergency.

The first ever ligatures for stitching wounds were made from human hair, horsehair or plant fibres such as flax or cotton. Silk was used for centuries until Joseph Lister, the 19th-century pioneer of antiseptic surgery, discovered that catgut produced much less inflammation. In doing so he resurrected a practice referred to by Galen in the 2nd century.

PASSING WATER

When it comes to health, the delicate matter of good, pain-free urination is one of the 'bodily functions' of abiding concern, and herbalists have long sought the perfect prophylactics and remedies for problems with passing water.

The dandelion, known to English country folk as 'piss-a-bed' and to the French as *pissenlit*, lives up to its reputation by being an effective diuretic – that is, it increases the flow of urine. In the 19th century both roots and leaves were essential ingredients of patent medicines sold to help flush out the kidneys and prevent gout (see page 134). It is the 'bitter principles'

During the severe rationing regimes of World War II ground, roasted dandelion root was used all over Europe as a substitute for coffee.

they contain that not only give dandeli-ons their distinctive taste (young leaves make an excellent salad) but also help to rid the body of excess water.

Anyone who has ever suffered from the pain of cystitis – infection of the urinary tract – will subscribe to the old adage that 'prevention is better than cure'. The fruit to the rescue is cranberry, a native of North American forests and bogs. A daily 'dose' of cranberry juice probably works by preventing bacteria from adhering to the cells that line the urinary tract.

Birch sap was probably already a well-known medicine when the Siennese physician Matthiolus claimed in 1565 that it would '… break the stone in the kidneys or bladder…' Country people extract this healing liquor in spring, before the tree breaks into leaf, by tapping the trunk.

NATURE'S PICK-ME-UPS
Feeling tired? Then the magic of ginseng may have the power to pick you up. Or recovery may come with help from the hedgerow.

The most ancient ginseng tonics were discovered thousands of years ago by the Chinese and made from the plant *Panax quinque-folius*, native to both China and North America. Its root, rather like a mandrake, looks like a wizened body, and its name comes from a Chinese word meaning 'root man'. The Chinese regard ginseng so highly that it has even been the cause of war, and smuggling the root was once punishable by death.

Betony (Stachys betonica), *believed to have been named for Beronice, whom Jesus healed of 'an issue of blood', has been revered since medieval times for its power to lift fatigue – and to keep away 'monstrous nocturnal visitors' and 'frightful visions and dreams'.*

For the most potent effects, the roots are gathered in the autumn from plants that are six to seven years old. (Siberian ginseng, also helpful for fatigue, is a totally different plant, *Eleutherococcus senticosus*, a thorny shrub whose roots contain substances that stimulate the immune system.)

Weary travellers might pick rose hips, fruits of the dog rose (*Rosa canina*) and boil them to make an invigorating syrup (now known to be packed with vitamin C). Or they might carry with them the mugwort plant (*Artemisia vulgaris*), whose juice could be drunk or, mixed with hog's fat, smeared on the feet to combat fatigue.

The herbalist William Coles wrote in 1656: 'If a footman take mugwort and put it in his shoes in the morning he may go forty miles before noon, and not be weary.'

GINSENG – FACTS AND FOLKLORE

- Wild ginseng roots are the most prized, identifiable by the 'stress rings' produced when the plant pushes through the soil.
- All ginseng roots were once considered the property of the Chinese emperor, who demanded, free of charge, a proportion of every crop.
- Ginseng comes to life in the shape of a 'trickster tree', which, when anyone tries to cut it down, pelts the woodcutter with tomato-sized berries.
- In North America the Iroquois prized ginseng, using it as both a medicine and an aphrodisiac.
- In Chinese thought the warmth of ginseng endows it with yang qualities.
- The scientific name Panax comes from 'panacea', meaning 'cure-all'.

AGAINST UNWELCOME WARTS

Warts – called verrucas when they grow on the soles of the feet – are caused by a virus. Before modern treatments were developed they were notoriously hard to shift, and there are dozens of old remedies for getting rid of them.

Both plants and animals feature abundantly in traditional wart remedies, which often specify exact circumstances for carrying out the treatment, such as a moonlit night. The juices of the celandine, dandelion and fig are believed to be especially efficacious.

Folk-Lore, a 1905 book about Shropshire customs, includes this typical remedy: 'Get up a plant of golden celandine at midnight under the moon. Bury it for three days – dig it up and squeeze the juice over the wart …' Cutting an apple in two and rubbing the pieces over a wart was also thought effective – as long as the two halves were afterwards reunited with string and the fruit buried. The idea was that as the apple rotted, so the warts would disappear. A potato could be used in the same way.

> *Other old ways of banishing warts are charming them, counting them and selling them to a friend.*

> *Animal blood, particularly that of moles, mice, pigs and cats, was commonly prescribed to help dispel warts. More evocative yet was this use of snails, described in 1873: 'Proceed this wise. Pierce the mollusc with a pin as many times as you have warts in number, then stick the snail on a blackthorn in the hedgerow; as the creature dies, so will the warts wane and disappear.' A toad was an effective snail substitute.*

WARTS AWAY

More plant and animal wart cures:

- *Cut as many notches in an elder stick (or hazel, ash, elm or oak) as you have warts and bury the stick.*
- *Rub the wart with the tail of a tortoiseshell tomcat (a very rare beast) – and only in the month of May.*
- *Tie a horse's hair around the wart.*
- *Put a live toad in a bag and carry it around your neck until the creature dies.*

FOR PROBLEM SKIN

Spots, itchiness, boils – these are just a few of the problems to which the skin is prone, and for which the plant world can still bring relief, as it has been doing for thousands of years.

The Egyptian pharaohs, so it is said, used the gel inside the fleshy leaves of *Aloe vera*, also known as the 'lily of the desert' and 'plant of immortality', to treat all kinds of skin problems, including burns and infections. The Greek herbalist Dioscorides, author of the 1st-century *De Materia Medica*, detailed its many uses: as well as soothing sunburn, itching and skin blemishes, these included everything from treating hair loss to mouth and gum disease. Legend has it that Aristotle persuaded Alexander the Great to conquer the island of Socotra off the east coast of Africa for the purpose of obtaining a sufficient quantity of *Aloe vera* to use as a healing agent for his soldiers' wounds.

It is said that aloe juice was used to preserve the body of Jesus after his crucifixion.

In times when everyone washed less, and antibiotic treatments were yet to be discovered, boils were commonplace and were often treated with hot poultices to bring them to a head. Chamomile flowers, boiled white lily roots and onion roots are among the poultice ingredients recommended by the Victorian handbook *Enquire Within*.

Even a lick from a healthy dog has been recommended to cure sores on the skin. The creature's tongue is said to possess curative properties.

The bark of the witch hazel (*Hamamelis virginiana*) helps the skin by calming inflammation and tightening up its tiny blood capillaries. In ancient times its reputation was assured by the fact that the flowers curl up like the snake which, as a symbol of wisdom, curls around the staff of Asclepius, the Greek god of medicine.

THE WORST ATTACKS

Unless an antidote is rapidly given, some snakebites can kill. Before modern remedies were available, the ancients had especially high regard for people with the power to extract the venom or nullify its effects.

The world's most potent animal venom comes from the scarlet poison-arrow frog, named for the traditional use of its poison by South American tribes. Just a millionth of a gram is enough to kill a human victim.

In the natural world, snakes use their poison to kill their prey, but when they are threatened they will attack and kill humans. Of those that bite, the cobras (and their close relatives the coral snakes) and the kraits are most deadly. The poison is usually injected via the reptiles' hollow fangs, quickly causing a burning sensation followed by paralysis, but Africa's spitting cobra, a killer marksman, literally spits its poison at its victims from a distance. The droplets can travel up to 8ft (2.5m), and just a gram of dried venom will kill over 160 people.

Reporting on written records of his time, Pliny tells of a 'race of men' who 'used to cure snake-bites by touch and extract the venom from the body by placing their hands on its surface'. He also mentions a near-extinct African tribe who 'produce in their bodies a poison deadly to snakes, and its odour puts snakes to sleep'.

For an adder bite, says Thomas Hardy in The Return of the Native, *'You must rub the place with the fat of other adders, and the only way to get that is by frying them.'*

In case of snakebite, don't attempt heroics by sucking out the venom. And don't try the old Somerset remedy of sucking the wound, spitting and chanting this rhyme three times:

Ashing tree, ashing tree,
Take this bite away from me.

An ancient remedy for a bite on the hand or foot was to kill a chicken and put the limb inside the bird's stomach. If, when the bird was cold, it turned black, this showed that the poison had passed from the victim into the bird.

TO EASE THE RHEUMATISM

Even our Neanderthal ancestors who lived some 50,000 years ago suffered from rheumatism and arthritis, which the ancient Egyptians called 'hardening in the limbs'.

Burdock, dandelion, flax, henbane, horse-radish and rosemary are among the herbs grown in medieval gardens and used to treat rheumatism. The leaves and bark of the ash tree, dubbed 'the quinine of Europe' are still used by modern herbalists. In America the plant Jeffersonia diphylla, *'rheumatism root', is similarly employed.*

An eelskin or snakeskin garter was once a popular anti-rheumatism accessory. The former were traditionally made in places such as the Fens of eastern England by a very complex method. First, eels were caught in the spring and their heads and tails cut off. The skins were left to dry in the sun, then softened with fat and stuffed with thyme and lavender. Over the summer they were buried in peat, between layers of mint, so that by the autumn, when damp and cold exacerbated aching joints, they were ready for wear. They were placed just above the knee, by men on the right leg and by women on the left.

Therapeutic stinging was common, and may well have worked because the stings stimulated blood flow to the affected part. A visit to a beekeeper for sting 'doses' was a traditional treatment for rheumatism, arthritis and neuritis. Testament to the longevity of this remedy is the fact that bee venom extract can still be purchased today. Thrashing the affected part with stinging nettles was a similar much-used treatment.

TO COOL A BURN

Though modern first aid for a burn is simple – put it under cold water and cover it loosely to avoid infection – treatments of the past involved a whole spectrum of natural remedies and even rhymes.

A typically complex ritual was used in Cornwall to soothe a burn. Nine bramble leaves were picked and floated in a basin filled, ideally, with water collected from a holy well (or failing that, pure spring water). The leaves were then passed, in turn, over and away from the affected area, while the healer chanted the rhyme:

Mixing elder tree 'rind' – the inner part of the bark – with butter, applying it to a burn, bandaging the area tightly and plunging the affected part into cold water is another old country remedy for burns, and may explain the old link (now discredited) between butter and burns.

> *There came three angels out of the east,*
> *One brought fire and two brought frost.*
> *Out fire, and in frost,*
> *In the name of the Father, Son and*
> *   Holy Ghost.*

Of the few herbal remedies still approved for burns today, the only one widely recommended is the soothing gel exuded by *Aloe vera* leaves. Used by the Egyptians (including, reputedly, Cleopatra) it is also thought to have been on board with Columbus during his voyages. Another succulent, the houseleek, is an old remedy for burns. Culpeper declared it 'good for all inward heats and out'. As a burn treatment the juice was often mixed with that of the plantain, or with cream.

BETTER MEMORIES

Nearly everyone would love a better memory – especially once they reach an age when memory lapses become more frequent. Herbal remedies have, for centuries, been recommended as memory improvers.

It is no accident that the ginkgo (*Ginkgo biloba*) is known by traditional Chinese doctors as 'the memory tree', for medical texts dating back to around 3000 BC state specifically that the tree's leaves will 'benefit the brain'. And indeed it does, probably by combating the deterioration in the circulation of blood to the brain that comes on with age.

In the eastern medical tradition of Ayurveda the herb gotu kola (Centella asiatica) is regarded as one of the most spiritual and rejuvenating herbs, helping to revitalize the nerves and brain cells and so improve the memory.

Sage (*Salvia officinalis*), whose common name is synonymous with wisdom, works by preventing the breakdown in the body of the substance acetylcholine, which is known to be essential to effective memory storage. This herb, sacred to the

Romans, was an obligatory ingredient in all kinds of concoctions, and was one of the herbs essential to the green pharmacopoeia of medieval monks. The 17th-century herbalist Nicholas Culpeper underlined its properties: 'Sage is of excellent use to help the memory,' he said, 'warming and quickening the senses.'

COPING WITH ALCOHOL

It is certain that for as long as people have enjoyed drinking alcohol they have looked for potions to prevent intoxication or relieve hangovers.

The oak tree is enshrined in the literature as a remedy 'against alcoholic excess'. It was recommended that a distilled spirit be made from acorns, which was said to 'help to control an abnormal craving for intoxicating liquors'. The onion, dubbed 'a drunkard's cure', was widely used, as was a hot drink called 'saloop', made from sassafras and served in 18th-century coffee houses.

Supping vinegar in which ivy berries had been dissolved before drinking and, afterwards, taking water in which bruised ivy leaves had been boiled, was a way of avoiding the ill effects of drink.

Bizarre remedies for a hangover involving the consumption of animals include the warm entrails of a freshly slaughtered sheep, favoured by the Greeks, and the fried canaries eaten by the Romans. In the 16th century a common cure was raw eels and almonds ground into a paste and eaten with bread. A live eel put into a drink was another suggestion.

In his Country Contentments *of 1633 Gervase Markham included a typical old herbal remedy: 'If you would not be drunke, take the powder of betony and coleworts [a kind of cabbage] mixt together; eate it every morning fasting, as much as will lie upon a sixpence, and it will preserve a man from drunkenness.'*

PREDICTIONS & SUPERSTITIONS

All kinds of animals and plants have been invoked over the ages to foretell the future, avert ill fortune and bring good luck. Their appearance and behaviour is believed to predict anything from the approach of bad weather to the character of a lover. And just carrying the image of an animal about your person, or keeping a lucky plant such as a four-leaved clover, may protect you from unforeseen dangers of many kinds.

On the basis that some animals may be witches or evil spirits in disguise, they need to be met, greeted and treated with respect – or summarily destroyed. There are countless stories and legends about such creatures, some of which were once thought to be servants of the gods. Among plants, deference is afforded to those with special symbolism, including the evergreens of Christmas whose all-year leafiness represents everlasting life. On all kinds of occasions, from getting married to setting off on a sea voyage, from giving birth to the rituals of death, the omens inherent in the natural world are deemed important; the many superstitions relating to such events clearly reflect the close link between human lives and those of plants and animals.

Though not real, the animal symbols seen in the constellations, and their changing positions relative to the sun and the planets, have for millennia been used to predict the fates of people born in different months or, according to the Chinese zodiac, different years. Whether we choose to believe the astrologers' predictions or not, the animal symbolism itself remains enormously powerful.

HARM THEM AT YOUR PERIL

Certain birds – and some insects – are so 'charmed' or sacred that causing harm to them in any way can bring disaster. Some of these creatures are also greatly feared.

Insects that should be afforded respect include ladybirds (ladybugs or ladybeetles). Dubbed by some 'God almighty's Cows', they should be released (or buried if accidentally killed) while chanting the rhyme: 'Ladybird, ladybird fly away home,/Your house is on fire and your children are gone.' It is also unlucky to kill an ant because it is said to embody the soul of an unbaptized child – or a fairy transformed into a human.

Deliberately killing a robin portends a life of doom. For a farmer it means that his cows will give bloody milk and his barns will catch fire. This is because the robin is revered as a bird with Christian connections (see page 35) and is believed to be protective and helpful, as in this ballad recounting the death of the Babes in the Wood:

Never kill a coyote or you may lose your wits. Killing a cat may shorten your life.

*No burial this pretty pair
From any man receives.
Till Robin Redbreast piously
Did cover them with leaves.*

Swans, associated in myth with the white clouds that formed the chariot of the Norse sun god Freyr, are deemed sacred throughout northern Europe. In Britain all swans are protected by law.

Swallows, who return year after year to the same nesting places in homes and barns, can consider themselves safe because it's believed that destroying their nests would bring harm to the buildings from fire or lightning. It is said that even cats know that it is unlucky to kill a swallow.

THE HELPFUL HORSE

The horse is an ancient Christian symbol of courage and generosity. It represents strength and fertility, and worldwide is linked with both life and death.

Until the 16th century it was customary to bleed horses for luck and health on St Stephen's Day, 26 December. To find out whether a mare was in foal the custom was to spit a mouthful of water into her ear as forcefully as possible. If in foal she would shake only her head, if not, her entire body.

The Norse god Odin rode through the heavens and across land and sea on Sleipnir, a white or dappled grey horse with eight legs.

Epona, the Celtic horse goddess, was worshipped as a bringer of fertility and the protector of the dead. Some believe that the Uffington white horse carving, created between 1400 and 600 BC on the chalk downland of southern England, is an image of the goddess.

For protection from the evil eye, horses' harnesses have long been adorned with brasses, brightly polished to shine light in the eyes of spirits and distract them. Popular motifs for the brasses include natural good luck symbols, such as the sun, crescent moon, acorn, heart, hand, bird and cat.

As a symbol of fertility the horse still appears as the hobbyhorse used in May Day ceremonials and in the horse's head staves carried by Morris dancers. In the USA and Europe, horses feature in the funeral rites of warriors and military commanders, with their boots symbolically set backwards into the stirrups.

LUCKY LEAVES

Clover and ferns are among the many leaves that can, in the right circumstances, bring good fortune. But they need to be kept or grown in specific ways to exert their powers benignly.

Finding a four-leaved clover – or in Ireland a shamrock – is the height of good fortune, as the old rhyme says: 'If you find a four-leaved clover/All your troubles will be over.' Country folk say that they grow where a mare has dropped her first foal. If you are extremely lucky you will meet your true love on the same day – and this special clover may even confer the gift of clairvoyance.

Rather than being carried in a pocket or purse, four-leaved clovers are believed to give the greatest protection against the Devil and his allies if pressed between the pages of a Bible or other valuable family book. Or they can be put into your right shoe or sewn inside your clothes.

Rare five-leaved clovers send mixed messages. Some say that finding one presages great wealth, others that it is a sign of impending sickness. Yet others believe it to be bad luck if found and kept but lucky if given to someone else.

FERN LORE
Like clovers, fern leaves work for good and ill:

• If a woman puts a fern leaf in her lover's shoe he will love her forever.

• If you wear a fern you will lose your way and be followed by snakes.

• If you bite the top off the first fern you see in spring it will keep you safe from toothache all year.

• Bunches of fern leaves put over a horse's ears or on its collar will deter the Devil and confuse witches.

• To keep away unwanted guests – and insects – cut and burn fern leaves on 30 July, the feast of St Abdon (the patron saint of cleanliness, who buried the bodies of early Christian martyrs), and scatter them around the house.

READING THE LEAVES

The tea leaves left in the bottom of your cup can reveal your personality – and even the future.

The time-honoured method of reading tea leaves is to invert your empty cup, having swirled it around three times, then place it on a saucer. The bottom of the cup is tapped with the index finger of the 'reader', who then picks up the cup and inspects it for signs to interpret. The practice reached the height of popularity in Britain in the late 1720s. In the 19th century amateur readers could make their interpretations with help from many books and articles on the subject.

For good luck, don't spill the milk you put in your tea, except if you are in Ireland, where such milk is believed to be the good fairies' favourite drink.

Be sure to put the lid on the pot or, it is said, you will need to call the doctor or will be visited by a stranger. Two people should never pour from the same pot. Another indication that a stranger is on the way is to find a tea leaf or stalk floating in your cup. Such a stalk is often called a 'beau'. If, when the tea is stirred, the beau clings to the spoon, the arrival of a male marriage partner is imminent.

YOUR FORTUNE IN TEA
Some common signs to be found in the cup:

Few leaves – *clarity of mind.*
Many leaves, spread out – *ambiguous: negligence but also generosity.*
Two parallel lines – *a journey.*
Star – *success, intelligence.*
Triangle – *jealousy, emotional involvement.*

Heart – *love, unless broken or crossed by a chain of leaves, when it means a broken love affair or divorce.*
Cross – *you are at the crossroads of life; a personal sacrifice may be necessary to resolve your problems.*
Dots – *letters on the way.*
Dashes – *surprises.*

ANIMAL TALISMANS

To keep death-dealing danger and the Evil Eye at bay, it has long been customary to wear a talisman or amulet bearing the image of a significant animal. The charm bracelet is a surviving form of such belief.

So widespread was the belief in the Evil Eye that prized livestock, including pigs and cattle, would also be provided with amulets to keep them free from harm.

A personification of 'the blighting glance of envy', the Evil Eye was much feared, particularly because it epitomized the idea of being 'overlooked'. An amulet was intended to attract the Evil Eye to itself and so protect the human who wore it. Frogs and scorpions were popular images, as were crocodiles, crabs, lions, dogs and ibises. On one ancient Greek example a man is being assailed by three scorpions, with a bird pecking his eye and a huge snake curled around his body. 'Envy, bad luck to you,' is the inscription, intended for any would-be evil doer.

As well as jewels and semi-precious stones, red or pink coral has been favoured for amulets, particularly to protect babies – hence its use in teething rings. In Africa elephant hairs are plaited into necklaces and bracelets. Sometimes the leaves or berries of poisonous plants such as woody nightshade would also be included, or plants such as betony that were known to have healing powers.

CHARMS ON THE BRACELET
These animal symbols may bring you good fortune:

Tortoise – *protection from evil*
Swallow – *general good luck*
Spider – *safety from illness*
Owl – *acquisition of knowledge*

Lion – *strength and bravery*
Fish – *wealth and fertility*
Eagle – *success for the ambitious*
Cat – *liberty*

DAYS OF THE KINGFISHER

The days of calm weather that usually descend on Europe around the end of the year are known as the halcyon days. And it is no coincidence that *Halcyon* is the scientific name of the kingfisher.

Halcyone was the daughter of Aeolus, Greek god of the four winds, and the wife of Ceyx, king of Thessaly, whom she dearly loved. On a sea journey to consult the oracle at Delphi, Ceyx was drowned when his ship was wrecked, and Halcyone was so stricken with grief that she jumped into the sea to be with her beloved. The gods took pity on the pair and changed them into kingfishers. What is more, to safeguard Halcyone's nest on the beach, Zeus declared that in their honour the winds of Aeolus should not blow for seven days before and seven days after the winter solstice, 21 December.

This period of calm is the time when Mediterranean kingfishers breed, and sailors say, 'So long as kingfishers are sitting on their eggs, no storm or tempest will disturb the ocean.' They are remembered in these lines from Milton's ode 'On the Morning of Christ's Nativity':

The kingfisher is a bird renowned for its darting dives and adeptness at catching fish. One legend says that when, during the flood, Noah was searching for land, the kingfisher was the second bird he sent out. But the foolish creature flew too high in the sky (which is why it has a blue back) and let the sun scorch its breast, turning it orange. Noah, in his irritation, made the bird stay on the ark thereafter, and dive into the water for food.

> *The winds with wonder whist [silent],*
> *Smoothly the waters kist,*
> *Whispering new joys to the mild ocean*
> *Who now hath quite forgot to rave*
> *While birds of calm sit brooding on the*
>   *charmed wave.*

PREDICTING STORMY WEATHER

Hovering close to the ocean surface, storm petrels look as though they are 'walking' on the waves, so they are often called St Peter's birds, because Peter followed Jesus's command to walk on water. Another theory is that the name comes from their 'pitter-pattering' on the water. They are also called 'Mother Carey's chickens', supposedly from the words 'Mater cara', or 'Dear mother', uttered by sailors when storms strike.

The behaviour of birds and animals has long been thought to predict the weather. When it comes to storms, the petrel and the cat take centre stage.

Except when they are breeding, many storm petrels (*Oceanites oceanicus*) live entirely at sea, feeding on plankton, krill and fish. To superstitious sailors, their appearance bodes ill, often rightly so, because they follow ships in stormy weather, scavenging for food scraps.

Both cats and petrels are widely be-lieved to take on the guise of witches and cause – and ride on – storms. To protect sailors, cats ashore would be shut up in cupboards. Even uttering the word 'cat' is still taboo among Scottish sailor folk.

CATS AT SEA
Some superstitions linking cats and storms:

- *Cats can start storms through magic stored in their tails, which is why sailors always make sure that they are well fed and contented.*
- *If a cat licks its fur against the grain a hailstorm is coming; if it sneezes, rain is on the way; and if it is frisky, the wind will soon get up.*
- *Throwing a cat overboard is a sure way of raising a storm.*
- *Fishermen's wives keep black cats at home to prevent storms and other disasters at sea.*

FLOWERS OF FATE

If you plan to bring flowers into the house, choose them with care or you may bring ill luck and even death in with them.

Be careful not to take home cut flowers that have been brought to you in hospital. If you do you will soon be back in hospital again. And avoid putting red and white blooms together – in Britain the combination signifies blood and bandages, and is said to augur doom.

The lilac, the fragrant flower of spring, is widely banned from the home as an unlucky cut flower with a 'drowsy scent', especially if white. This superstition may spring from the legend of the girl who died the night before her marriage but not before requesting that lilacs be planted on her grave. When they bloomed their flowers were white.

Though a symbol of the hope that comes with the spring, the snowdrop, because it grows so close to the ground, is said to be more attached to the dead than the living, and is thought to look like a corpse in its shroud. For both these reasons it is regarded as a death omen if picked and brought indoors. By tradition, the single snowdrop is the most unlucky. The lone violet has a similarly morbid reputation. Primroses, especially in a bunch of fewer than 13 blossoms, are also unwelcome in the house, and should never be given as a gift.

As well as being fatal to humans, cut primroses are regarded by country folk as the surest way to prevent chicks from hatching or to cause young hens to die.

SAFE AT HOME

The plants that grow on and around the home – our precious refuge – have long been chosen with care to keep us safe from attack by everything from fire to evil spirits. But there are some things that should never be brought indoors.

Peacock feathers shouldn't be brought into the house. They are said to bear the colours of the seven deadly sins. When God created the bird, so the story goes, the sins were jealous of its beauty. As punishment, God removed the yellow eye of envy, the green eye of jealousy, the red eye of murder – and all the rest – and put them into the peacock's tail. The sins themselves followed, in their vain attempt to regain the eyes they had lost.

The houseleek (*Sempervivum tectorum*), whose scientific name combines the Latin words for 'everlasting' and 'on a roof' was originally planted on the roofs of houses for the practical reason of preventing the tiles from slipping, but it has long been thought to protect a home from being burnt down or struck by lightning, as well as from evil spirits and the ravages of disease. The medieval emperor Charlemagne even passed a law that houseleeks should be grown on the roof of every dwelling.

Wall rue (*Asplenium ruta-muraria*), a small fern that commonly grows in tufts embedded in the crevices and joints of walls, was thought lucky because it kept witches at bay. A bonus was that it could be used to help cure rickets, a disease once known as 'the taint'. This explains its old name of 'tentwort'.

A LUCKY HOME

To protect your home from being struck by lightning – *hang a laurel wreath on the door or plant an olive or a hawthorn tree in the garden.*
To keep away evil spirits – *plant cloves of wild garlic in the thatch over a doorway or hang them indoors.*
To keep witches at bay – *stick pins into a bull's heart and place it in the chimney.*
To preserve good fortune – *if a butterfly enters, shut the windows and doors to stop it escaping.*

ANIMALS AT HOME

From snakes to sparrows, creatures that come into the home can presage good or ill, depending on their identity and the way they behave.

In countries where they are indigenous, snakes that come into the house are generally thought to be lucky. As well as generally bringing good fortune, they are believed to embody the souls of ancestors, and to be guardian spirits that watch over the members of the family, especially children. In Armenia a snake that arrives in the night is offered food and drink – the hospitality any stranger would be afforded. Similarly, the sudden departure of a house snake is said to presage misfortune. The sloughed skin of a snake, hung up in the house, is thought to make it fireproof.

Welcome rooks who nest in trees near your home – they are said to bring good luck; but beware if they desert their rookery, for then bad luck may befall.

Like house snakes, sparrows may also contain the souls of the departed. If they fly into the house they are said to presage death. That sparrows should be treated with caution is summed up in the old rhyme: 'The spink [chaffinch] and the sparrow/Are the Devil's bow and arrow.'

AROUND THE MAYPOLE

Ensuring fertility – of crops, cattle and humans – was the original purpose of dancing around the maypole on May Day. The tree that forms the pole represents the spirit of the forest springing back to life.

Even before maypoles were erected on village greens in Celtic times, decorated with garlands and flowers to make them look 'alive', the Greeks are known to have celebrated the festival of Daidala in an ancient oak forest in Plataea. First, cooked meat was set out on the ground, to attract birds. The tree chosen for cutting was the one on which the first bird with this food in its mouth was seen to alight. After being felled, the tree was carved into the effigy of a woman dressed as a bride and carried in procession in honour of the goddess Hera.

The birch, renowned for being able to avert the Evil Eye, is greatly favoured as a maypole, and dancing around the flower-decked maypole is an integral part of the English May Day ritual. The ribbons on the pole, which the dancers weave as they dance in opposing circles, were introduced by John Ruskin in the 19th century. In Germany, desirable foods such as sausages were traditionally hung on the maypole, and young men climbed up it to win them.

Describing his delight at first seeing a maypole in 1820, the American author Washington Irving wrote: 'The mere sight of this May-Pole gave a glow to my feelings, and spread a charm over the country for the rest of the day …'

BRINGING HOME THE MAY

Not only the maypole is garlanded on May Day – the May Queen and King are also adorned with blooms and leaves. To secure good fortune for the year, May boughs were cut on May Day eve or early in the morning of the day itself.

'Bringing home the May' symbolizes the arrival of new life. Garlands made from the greenery collected were traditionally carried in procession or taken from door to door, as a way of sharing the earth's newly sprung fertility – it was bad luck to refuse to give money to 'remember the garland'.

On 1 May the prettiest girl in the village is chosen as the May Queen or Bride and sits near the maypole swathed in flowers, especially May blossom. Wreathed in greenery (usually oak and hawthorn boughs) with only his face visible, the May King, also known as Jack-in-the-Green, first feigns death then jumps up to dance with her, mimicking nature's renaissance. In some places, the wrists of the May sovereigns are bound together, also with a garland.

THE MAY – FLOWER OF MIXED FORTUNES

May is the common name for haw-thorn blossom, which brings good luck when it is used outdoors in May festivities but bad luck when cut and brought indoors.

To the Greeks the May (*Crataegus monogyna*) was a flower of great fortune, and a symbol of luck for newly-weds. May blossoms were often held over a couple as they wed, the bride wore them in her headdress, the altar was strewn with them and torches made from haw-thorn wood were lit to guide the pair to their nuptial chamber.

The ritual of gathering the May is

thought to date back to the annual Roman rite of honouring Flora, the goddess of flowering plants. The conjugal connotations were celebrated by many poets, typified by these lines from a 19th-century verse by John Ingram:

The hawthorn's bloom is falling, love,
We must no longer wait;
Each bird is blithely calling, love,
Unto his chosen mate …

That it is unlucky to bring May blossoms indoors because it will presage death may stem from the pungent odour of the blooms, said to be like that of the plague. Children are particularly discouraged from the practice, being told that it would kill their mothers.

FLOWERS OF ST JOHN'S EVE

In the country calendar, 23 June, the eve of the festival of St John the Baptist, is a night when witches are thought to ride abroad. They must be deterred with the help of protective plants if cattle, crops and people are to thrive until harvest time. Though the summer solstice is on 21 June, St John's Day is traditionally celebrated as Midsummer Day. Special to this festival is St John's wort (*Hypericum perforatum*), a yellow-flowered plant with a pungent smell generated by the oil glands in its leaves, and whose red spots symbolize the spilled blood of the saint. When burnt on the Midsummer bonfire this oil scented the smoke, through which people had to jump to insulate themselves against evil. It was also often hung on doors and windows and placed around the home for protection.

PRESERVED FOR
FORTUNE AND HEALTH

As well as St John's wort, other flowers were preserved on St John's Eve and hung around the house and cowshed to keep illness and evil at bay. These included:

Vervain (verbena) – *long believed to be magical and holy, and to have healing powers.*

Mugwort – *protective against both witches and thunder.*

Yarrow – *strewn on a threshold to keep witches at bay.*

Elder – *given to the bewitched to break the spell and restore them to health.*

Male fern (especially the root, which looks like a gnarled hand) – *used to protect a household and their livestock from demons, witchcraft and the Evil Eye.*

A GOOD DEATH

According to ancient superstitions, the way in which animals and plants are involved at the time of a death will affect the fate of those left behind – including family pets.

One of the events deemed most unlucky is for a cat or dog to leap over a corpse, which will turn it into a vampire and could also make the next person it leaps over go blind.

It is an old custom is to tell the news of a death to the birds and bees. Rooks, lucky when they nest near the home, need the information to make sure that they stay put. For a similar reason, someone from the family should go to the beehive, tap three times and say, 'Little brownie, little brownie, your master's dead.' They then need to wait to hear the bees hum, to

> *Bees were often also presented with food from the funeral meal to keep them totally involved in the proceedings.*

> *To ensure that plants and pet birds continued to thrive after a death, pots and cages were ritually tied with black crape following a death in the family.*

signify that they are happy to remain.

To be doubly sure that the bees did not depart it was common for their hives to be lifted and turned at exactly the moment the coffin was lifted on to the hearse.

THE PLANTS OF THE GRAVEYARD

The plants that grow in a graveyard, from yew trees to grass, have long been associated with magical, mystical and even healing powers. Disturbing a graveyard's flora attracts great misfortune.

Even the grass that grows in a graveyard can be propitious. One Welsh story relates how a woman bitten by a mad donkey was sent to a churchyard to eat grass, which would cure her. A potion made from boiled nettles gathered from a graveyard is said to be a cure for dropsy.

The yew, long revered for its ability to protect against evil, and a symbol of life after death, is a tree widely associated with burial grounds, and many English yews are thought to be older than the churches they grow by. To cut down a churchyard yew, or even to burn or damage it in any way, is believed to presage ill fortune, though sprigs of yew were once put into a dead person's shroud, and branches were carried by mourners before being put into the grave with the coffin.

Moss taken from a graveyard headstone can, it's said, cure illness, especially in animals. And nearby animals may suffer from death and illness if a grave is disturbed.

After burial, prickly brambles were traditionally planted around the edge of the grave to keep the Devil out and to protect the soul of the departed from escaping. Monkey puzzle trees, with their hugely thorny leaves, are planted in graveyards to prevent the Devil from hiding in the branches and watching the funeral from above.

ANIMAL NAMES – THE BAD AND THE GOOD

In dangerous situations even the names of certain animals should never pass the lips. To say them is to invite ill luck or, at worst, death itself.

For the best of luck on the first of the month you should, say 'Hares' or 'Black rabbits' when you go to bed the night before and 'Rabbits' or 'White rabbits' when you wake up in the morning. Don't make the mistake of saying 'Black rabbits' then, or luck will very soon desert you.

Regarding creatures' names – and indeed the animals themselves – sailors and fishermen are by far the most superstitious. At sea, for instance, a pig will be referred to as 'the thing' (as it will by friends and relatives while someone close is out on the ocean). Similarly rabbits and hares are called 'those hairy things'. Should anyone on board speak the animal's actual name a crew might well turn back to shore immediately for fear of being shipwrecked.

The cat is another animal not mentioned by name on board ship, though to have a truly black cat, without a single white hair, is lucky at sea. Miners also avoid saying the word 'cat', and will even kill one they find underground. In the theatre a cat is lucky as long as it is not kicked and is prevented from running across the stage.

Be very afraid: *on the Isle of Portland in Dorset, the word 'rabbit' is so feared that it is never even said – or even printed in the local newspaper. To put an evil spell on someone, the words 'Rabbits to you' are said to be horrifyingly effective.*

BIRDS OF DOOM

Once revered as messengers of the gods, and endowed with powers of flight denied to mere mortals, birds and their behaviour have strong links

with the foretelling of death. **The ways in which birds behave around a home are, to the superstitious, significant death predictors.**

Most to be feared are a bird that flies into the house through an open window or down the chimney, a bird tapping on the window or one hovering over the house. You also need to listen for the calls that birds make, especially at unusual times. Cocks crowing late at night, ravens croaking between 10 o'clock and midnight and a cuckoo that calls after August are all believed to presage death.

> *Two large white birds, the size and shape of albatrosses, are said to fly over Salisbury Cathedral when the death of the incumbent bishop is imminent.*

Certain places and families have had particular reasons to fear the appearance of birds. The Oxenham family of Devon long believed that when someone fell ill they would be sure to die if a white-breasted bird appeared in the bedroom and hovered over the sick bed before disappearing.

The numbers and positions in which birds are seen can be significant. Single magpies ('One for sorrow'), while generally unlucky, are not as bad as a whole flock seen flying past the house. A single white pigeon on a roof is a death omen, as are three seagulls seen flying close together.

MORE AVIAN OMENS
Expect a death in the family if:

- *A swallow alights on you.*
- *A pigeon settles on your kitchen table.*
- *You meet a vulture.*
- *Hens lay eggs with double yolks.*
- *A cock crows all day and night.*

ENSURING CONCEPTION

The desire for fertility was especially strong when medicine was less sure and the hold on life more precarious. It was only natural to look to the living world for signs and symbols that ensure conception.

You may need to be careful what you keep about your person. For, as Pliny the Roman naturalist said, 'Mistletoe ... will promote conception in females if they make a practice of carrying it about in their pockets'.

The crops of certain plants were seen as significant to fertility, and abundant crops of nuts and apples were once said to be 'good for children', while an ash tree that failed to bear its winged fruits or 'keys' was a sure sign that few children would be born the following year.

What a woman eats may be significant, too. It is an old country belief that lettuce could make women barren and men sterile. Consuming parsley was thought to have similar effects, though by contrast planting parsley seeds was a sure way to become pregnant. The mandrake (see page 73) has been revered since Biblical times for its power to bring about conception. The Old Testament tells of barren Rachel becoming pregnant by this means. However even the medieval herbalists were sceptical and the selling of mandrake roots for this purpose was condemned in the 17th century by Sir Thomas Browne as a trick against 'ignorant people' and a way 'to deceive unfruitful women'.

FRUITS FOR FERTILITY

In the green world, several trees and their fruits have become symbols of fertility and acquired reputations as aphrodisiacs.

Its many fleshy seeds – each said to represent one child – make the pomegranate a fertility symbol.

The fig, *with its fruits shaped like sexual organs, has a reputation as both an aphrodisiac and a fertility symbol, and in some African countries the fig tree is regarded as the spiritual husband of barren women. Quinces, revered in ancient Greece, were eaten by brides to ensure that they would bear children.*

According to myth, the tree grew from the blood shed by the hermaphrodite monster Agdistis when it lost its male parts to become the Phrygian mother goddess Cybele. Some of the tree's fruits were picked by a river nymph. One fruit disappeared, and the girl discovered she was pregnant and gave birth to the god Attis, who became Cybele's lover.

Carrying a pomegranate or a pine cone are old ways of ensuring fertility. The pine cone's phallic shape made it an obvious selection as a symbol of life and in various places the pine is planted as a 'wedding tree' that will bring many children. In ancient Mesopotamia the pine cone was the emblem of Marduk, the chief god of the Babylonians.

FRUITFUL SYMBOLS

The forms of certain plants and flowers make them obvious fertility symbols:

Mistletoe – *highly regarded because it bears its succulent-looking fruits in midwinter.*

Acorn – *like the pine cone, a phallic symbol.*

Lotus – *revered because it opens with the sun in the morning and closes at night.*

Orchid – *a plant with overtly sexual flower formations.*

Peony – *an emblem of feminine beauty, traditionally worn by a bride to ensure that she will bear many children.*

AN EASIER BIRTH

From the days when it was believed that witches worked their evil at childbirth, harming both mother and baby, many superstitions are associated with the moment of birth.

The skin of a snake has long been thought to ease childbirth and ease the pain. A record of 1897 called *Lying Prophets* describes how a woman 'picked up the adder's slough, designing to sew it upon a piece of flannel and henceforth wear it against her skin until her baby should be born …'

According to a seemingly farfetched Scandinavian belief, a woman can avoid the pain of childbirth by crawling naked through the caul (membrane) in which a newborn foal was encased. However, if she does this, her first child will be a werewolf if it is a boy and a succubus (a female demon) if a girl. The only way to lift the curse is for the child – who can be detected by a hairy lump on the shoulder – to eat the heart of an unborn baby.

Named because they drift from the Molucca islands on to the beaches of Scotland's western isles, molucca or Virgin Mary beans (especially white ones) were once used as amulets to help women 'travailing in childbirth'.

WHERE CHILDREN COME FROM

We have all heard tales of 'the birds and the bees' – the euphemistic terms for sex. But why were children told they were brought by storks or found by their parents under a gooseberry bush?

Modesty to the point of prudishness was, in a bygone age, the chief reason for disguising the facts of life. The stork was probably given its symbolic role because of its meticulous parenting as well as its habit of nesting on house roofs. It was an ancient belief that storks picked up babies from marshes, ponds and springs, where the souls of unborn infants resided. In Germany and other parts of Europe, seeing a stork flying over a house is a sign of an impending birth.

The notion that newborn babies may be found 'under a gooseberry bush' links human fertility with that of the earth. The parsley bed is another place where children may be found because of the links between this herb and fertility and health. An old country custom to ensure that a child had good eyesight was to collect rainwater during a thunderstorm, steep parsley in it and then use the liquid to bathe the eyes of a newborn.

WHO'LL BE MY LOVE?

There are countless ways in which would-be lovers have tried to conjure up an image or find the identity of a future partner, with rituals using everything from flowers to apple pips.

It was the custom for country girls to pick heads of rye grass and, as they touched each of the seeds growing up the stem, chant: 'Tinker, tailor, solider, sailor, rich man, poor man, beggar man, thief.' The last seed revealed what kind of man they would marry.

Tisty-tosties – balls made from cowslips – were tossed between the young who, all the while, spoke a hurried list of the names of possible contenders for their favours. The name still on the lips at the moment the ball was dropped was 'the one'. Though this game was usually played between girls, boys might also be involved, or so this verse by Robert Herrick suggests:

I call, I call. Who do ye call?
The maids to catch this cowslip ball;
But since these cowslips fading be,
Troth, leave the flowers; and maids, take me.
Yet, if that neither you will do,
Speak but the word, and I'll take you.

To make a tisty-tosty, cowslip flowerheads were picked off close to the top of the stalks and 50 to 60 of them were hung along a string. The flowers were then pushed carefully together and the string tied tightly to gather them into a ball.

APPLE DIVINATION

There are lots of ways to use an apple to predict your romantic future:

• Throw apple pips representing your would-be lovers into the fire and say 'If you love me, pop and fly/If you hate me, lay and die.'
• Squeeze an apple pip between finger and thumb and shoot it, chanting: 'Kernel come kernel, hop over my thumb,/ And tell me which way my true love will come,/East, west, north, or south,/Kernel jump into my true love's mouth.'
• Chant the alphabet as you twist off an apple stalk. Your love's name will have the initial you are saying as the stalk comes off.
• Throw the peel of an apple, pared off entire, over your shoulder – or hang it on a nail on the door – and it will form the initial of your future love.

ANIMAL LOVE SIGNS

Depending on how and when you meet them and the way they behave, animals, too, may predict the course of true love.

The ladybird (or ladybug), which 'flies away home', is also believed to take wing to a true love. When you find the insect it should be gently blown off the hand or tossed into the air while chanting the words:

Fly away east, fly away west,
Show me where lives the one I love best.

Alternatively, you can use this old rhyme:

Bishop, Bishop Barnabee,
Tell me when my wedding be;
If it be tomorrow day,
Take your wings and fly away.

A bizarre old custom is throwing a herring membrane. Along the underside of the fish is a small strip of fat. A girl would remove this and throw it at a wall. If it landed upright, then her husband would be equally admirable, but a membrane that landed in a crooked fashion denoted a dishonest partner.

On St Valentine's Day, young women would peer through the keyhole of the house. If they saw a cock and a hen they could be sure to be wed within the year. In spring, they would count the calls of the first cuckoo, the number of calls being the years until marriage.

Even snails can be called on for the purposes of divination. When every home had an open fire, Shropshire girls were advised: 'Take a black snail by the horns, and throw it over your shoulder on to the hearth at night. In the morning, its slimy trail among the ashes will show the initials of your future husband.'

CREATURES OF CHRISTMAS LORE

Animals may augur good luck or bad at Christmas time. They play an important part in many of the ancient Christmas customs, and it is a widespread belief that the descendants of those who were

present at the Nativity still show their deference on Christmas night.

Christmas Eve, and twelve of the clock.
'Now they are all on their knees,'
An elder said as we sat in a flock
By the embers in hearthside ease.

We pictured the meek mild creatures where
They dwelt in their strawy pen,
Nor did it occur to one of us there
To doubt they were kneeling then.

Bees hum a sacred hymn on Christmas Eve. After the calendar changed by 11 days in 1752 (not to everyone's pleasure) people would listen on both the 'old' and 'new' Christmas to make sure they could hear it – and to reveal the 'true' date of Christmas.

So Thomas Hardy viewed the kneeling of the cattle in midnight homage; their breath is averred to be sweet because it warmed the infant Jesus. Sheep, also, are said to turn to the east and bow at this hour, and it is deemed especially lucky to meet a flock at this time of year. The power of the crowing cock to dispel evil spirits which, like the ghost of Hamlet, fade 'on the crowing of he cock', is particularly potent at Christmas, when it is said to raise its voice all night long.

Old Christmas country rituals involved parading animal effigies in the streets. In Dorset (where it was called the Ooser) and Wiltshire, a terrifying bull's head mask was worn by a man swathed in sacking, who demanded refreshment from anyone he met. In Kent a horse's head on a pole was paraded, demanding drinks and money: 'If ye the hooden horse doth feed,/Throughout the year thou shalt not need.'

Even to talk of a wolf during the 12 days of Christmas may bring bad luck.

One of the oldest Christmas foods is the roast pig served with an apple in its mouth. This tradition goes back to the pig called a *julgalti*, offered to the Norse god Freyr to ensure fertility in the year to come.

O CHRISTMAS TREE!

Until it was introduced from Germany by Prince Albert, the Christmas tree was virtually unknown in Britain, though the tradition of bringing evergreens indoors at this season goes back to ancient pagan festivals.

One possible origin for the custom of decorating trees for Yule relates to legends that certain trees burst into bloom on Christmas Day. One was the miraculous Glastonbury thorn, believed to have sprung from the staff of Joseph of Arimathea who, on his mission to Britain, planted it in the ground on Christmas Eve. Such flowering trees were especially revered in Germany. In 1430 one writer recorded that: 'Not far from Nuremburg there stood a wonderful tree. Every year, in the coldest season, on the night of Christ's birth this tree put forth blossoms and apples as thick as a man's thumb. This in the midst of deep snow and in the teeth of cold winds.'

The Yule log represents the fires lit in the pre-Christian midwinter festival of the same name, at which gifts were exchanged.

Lights on the Christmas tree illuminate the dark days of winter as well as the advent of the 'Light of the world'. Legend has it that it was Martin Luther who first decorated a tree with candles.

Trees were cut and used in plays performed at Christmas, telling the whole Christian story from Adam and Eve to the Resurrection. In this context the Christmas tree represented both the Tree of Knowledge and Christ's Cross.

CHRISTMAS EVERGREENS

The holly, ivy and mistletoe are the quintessential Christmas evergreens, and all must be handled correctly to avoid ill fortune. They must certainly be removed by 6 January, which is Twelfth Night or the feast of the Epiphany.

By old country lore, while the prickly holly represents the male, the ivy is undoubtedly feminine. The Greeks called it cissos *after a dancing girl who danced herself to death at the feet of Dionysus and was transformed into the plant by the god, so moved was he by her art. Unlike holly, ivy is not always welcomed indoors, but kept for decorating doorways and porches 'just in case'.*

For their Christmas celebrations, early Christians adapted the traditions of the bawdy Roman midwinter festival of Saturnalia, and brought in evergreens to decorate their homes and churches. Christmas Eve is the most propitious day for cutting greenery; if you use it before this date quarrels are sure to ensue.

Mistletoe, revered by the Druids and used on their altars, was originally hung up at Christmas to confer divine protection from fire, injury and all other ills and to drive away evil spirits. It was even hung in cowsheds to ensure the continued health of the livestock. It is, however, never seen inside a church.

MISTLETOE LORE

- When a man kisses his would-be love he must pluck a berry and present it to her. Only if she accepts it will her love be true.
- Keep the mistletoe all year and burn it before the new sprigs are put up. A good sign is a steady flame; a spluttering one means a bad-tempered husband.
- You will stay unmarried for the year if you are not kissed under the mistletoe.
- After being kissed a girl should pick a mistletoe leaf, and a berry. In the privacy of her room she must swallow the berry and prick on to the leaf the initials of the man she loves then stow the leaf as near to her heart as possible.

EASTER RITES

The original 'Easter bunny' was in fact a hare. The link goes back to pre-Christian times, when this creature was sacred to the Anglo-Saxon goddess Eastre, after whom the festival was named.

Once revered as holy, the hare was associated with fertility and the return of spring, by tradition it is the hare that lays the brightly coloured eggs hidden for children to hunt for on Easter morning. The benevolence of the hare at this season was at odds, however, with the widely held idea that hares were witches in disguise. It was extremely unlucky to meet one and to do so was even thought to put you into severe danger.

The flowers of Easter are the daffodil and the Easter lily, the latter is often used in church decorations to commemorate the departed of previous fill text years.

The fernlike leaves of the tansy (Tanacetum), a plant with yellow, button-like flowers, were an essential ingredient of the 'tansies' once eaten during Lent and at Eastertide. These were a kind of pancake consumed in imitation of the bitter herbs eaten by Jews at Passover.

At their spring festivals the ancient Greeks and Romans exchanged coloured eggs and today hard-boiled, painted eggs (dyed red in some countries to signify the spilt blood of Christ) still represent Easter's promise. One Polish legend relates that eggs were first painted by Mary to amuse the infant Jesus. Easter eggs are put into the fields to encourage good crops and protect them from hail and thunder, and in some places one may be kept in the house as a protective amulet.

HARVEST TIME

To ensure a good harvest, grain must be properly sown and certain rituals observed when it is ripe, many of which go back countless generations.

The cock is often believed to be a protective 'corn spirit'. This explains why straw models of cocks were once placed at the ends of ricks. They served the same purpose as corn dollies, effigies (originally of the corn goddess Demeter, whose spirit was thought to reside in the corn) woven from the last ears of the harvest and ploughed into the earth the following spring.

When bringing in the harvest it is an old good luck custom to include the corn dolly in the final load, which is decked with flowers, ribbons or branches. On the way back from the fields the workers sing:

> *Harvest home! Harvest home!*
> *We've ploughed, we've sowed,*
> *We've reaped, we've mowed,*
> *And brought safe home*
> *Every load.*

A bunch of hops from the harvest, kept over the hearth or chimney, will bring good luck to the home for a twelve-month. It must, however, be replaced each year.

Red poppies and green bindweed adorned the rush hat of the harvest lord. He was the man who set the working pace of the harvest, and could fine anyone who hindered the proceedings by, for example, letting out chickens into uncut corn.

SOW AND TREAT IT RIGHT

To ensure an abundant crop of corn:

- *Along with your wheat, plant some twigs that have been blessed on Palm Sunday.*
- *Present any stranger who visits the wheat field with a nosegay of flowers.*
- *Avoid ploughing on Good Friday if you want your wheat to germinate.*
- *Sow all the seed you take to the field and scatter it with ashes from fires lit on Midsummer Eve.*
- *To deter rats in the granary, hang up a hot cross bun kept from Good Friday.*
- *Cut the corn with a flail that has a handle of holly or a hawthorn.*

NATURE AT HALLOWEEN

All Hallows' Eve, 31 October, is a day on which it is essential to foster good luck, for this is when witches and ghosts are abroad.

Pumpkins are hollowed out and lit at Halloween because they are symbols of both fertility and protection. The original intention of putting candles inside was to drive away evil spirits. Most protective of all are those fruits grown from seeds planted on Good Friday. Hanging garlic in the house will also keep evil spirits away.

Halloween is a date for divination. On this night it is an old ritual for girls to go blindfold into the garden and pull up a cabbage. A well-grown vegetable is a promise of a handsome husband but one with a crooked stalk is an omen of a crooked, stingy mate. A cabbage with a club root presages a man with a similar deformity.

At Halloween, each family member takes an ivy leaf, marked with their name, and puts it in a bowl of water. If, by the morning, the mark has turned into the shape of a coffin, their death is imminent.

According to Irish lore, to dream of his love on Halloween a man should pick ten ivy leaves and put nine of them under his pillow. Wreaths of ivy placed on graves at Halloween protect the souls of the departed.

HALLOWEEN PREDICTIONS

- *If you can catch a falling leaf before it reaches the ground you can have a wish.*
- *Two people each put a chestnut into the fire. The person whose nut bursts first will be the first to be married.*
- *Put a snail into an enclosed box overnight and its trail will spell out the initial of your lover.*
- *A fire lit at Halloween will protect cattle over the winter.*

A LUCKY MARRIAGE

Every bride and groom wishes for good luck, and many country superstitions contribute to an auspicious wedding day.

As with other important family events, it is essential to a happy marriage to tell the good news to the bees before the event, ideally dressed in one's best. The bees should be invited to the ceremony and allowed to share in the feast by being offered a piece of wedding cake.

Rice, wheat and almonds thrown over the newly wed bride and groom are all ancient fertility symbols. Rose petals – either real or paper – should also confer a life of love.

Wedding flowers traditionally include roses, the pre-eminent floral love symbols. Adding sprigs of rosemary will also bring luck and, as a guest, you can invoke both luck and love by putting rosemary in your pocket. At ancient weddings myrtle wreaths were worn by both bride and groom as symbols of love and peace, and this plant can also be included in the bridal flowers.

Animals met on the way to a wedding can also influence fortune. It is lucky for a bride to meet a horse, and for a horse and rider to be the first thing the couple see after the service. It is also lucky to have a toad walk across their path or for a dove to fly overhead. In the East, meeting an elephant is especially propitious.

WHO WILL BE THE BOSS?
A woman will dominate the home if:

- *Holly brought in at Christmas is smooth, not prickly.*
- *Parsley grows profusely, because 'Where parsley grows faster, the mistress is master'.*
- *Rosemary flourishes in the garden, because this means 'the grey mare is the better horse'.*

MONEY AND WEALTH

Nearly all of us wish, if not for wealth, at least for enough money to be 'comfortable'. If you read the signs of the natural world correctly, riches may indeed come your way.

For money, have a bee land on your hand. However, it is bad luck to exchange bees for money: they must be lent, or swapped for 'goods in kind'. And if stolen, they will never thrive.

When you hear the first cuckoo call of the season turn the money in your pocket and spit on it. And remember the old saying, 'Who eats oysters on St James's Day will never want.' (The saint's day, 25 July, once marked the beginning of the oyster season.)

Animals you encounter can also confer wealth. A frog is a sign of money (in Scotland a prudent housewife might even keep one in the cream bowl). And if, on the way to conduct important business, a black and white spotted dog crosses your path, you will meet with success. If you see the first lamb of spring facing you, it signifies a diet of meat for the rest of the year – and the money to afford it. But if you see the creature's tail first you will eat only milk and vegetables. Similarly, if the first butterfly you see in spring is white then you will eat white bread for the rest of the year. Conversely, a brown butterfly means brown bread, traditionally associated with poverty.

MORE LUCKY SIGNS

Expect money to come your way if:

- You see a ladybird with many spots. The number of spots was once said to equal the number of shillings a farmer could charge for a bushel of wheat.
- A money spider runs over your clothes.
- Swallows nest on your house, especially near a window.
- You see cranes flying in the sky – you will gain money and status.
- You hear your first cuckoo on 28 April.

KILLED FOR GOOD?

While it is generally bad luck to harm any animal, there are some well-known instances in which killing a creature may be necessary to ensure good fortune.

Millers would kill a cock at midnight on St Martin's Eve (10 November) and sprinkle its blood over their machinery. This custom of 'blooding the mill' was believed to protect the miller from accidents in the following year. To protect farmers' livelihoods nightjars were once shot with a silver sixpence loaded into a gun – no other ammunition would do. These birds, whether or not they were witches in disguise, were traditionally loathed because they were reputed to suck goats' udders, making them blind and infecting them with disease.

It is deemed advisable to kill the first butterfly you see in spring to prevent it from 'haunting' you – because it is a malign soul or a ghost. Seeing one at night, at any time of year, is a warning of death and its demise is justifiable.

FOR HUMAN PROTECTION

Unfortunate creatures may meet their ends for many reasons:

- *A white cricket on the hearth – because it is an omen of death.*
- *A sparrow you have caught – or your parents will not survive.*
- *A dog with rabies (hydrophobia). For fear of a mad dog's deadly bite, any hound that howled on Christmas Eve was once killed quickly and unceremoniously.*
- *A snake you meet on your path (except the first adder of spring). Certain rhymes said under the breath can make them twist themselves into suicidal knots.*

THE LUCKY GREETING

Meeting – and greeting – animals and birds may bring good luck, depending on how you do it.

Old superstitions often demand the reciting of verse, or even elaborate actions to ward off evil.

The evil powers of bats, widely viewed as agents of death and the Devil, or witches in disguise, certainly need to be assuaged. One old way is to chant a protective verse such as:

> Dispel the bad luck of a crow by saying, 'Crow, crow, get out of my sight/Or else I'll eat thy liver and lights.'

> *Airy mouse, airy mouse fly over my head,*
> *And you shall have a crust of bread;*
> *And when I brew and when I bake,*
> *You shall have a piece of my wedding cake.*

The magpie, said to be coloured black and white because it refused to go into full mourning after the Crucifixion, may be unlucky or the reverse, according to the old rhyme (which has several versions):

> *One for sorrow, two for mirth,*
> *Three for a wedding, four for a birth,*
> *Five for silver, six for gold,*
> *Seven for a secret, not to be told,*
> *Eight for heaven, nine for Hell*
> *And ten for the Devil's own sell [self].*

There are many traditional ways of dispelling the ill luck of seeing one magpie. You may, bow and say aloud 'Good morning to you Mr Magpie, Sir,' or 'Good magpie, magpie, chatter and flee, turn up thy tail and good luck fall me.' You may remove your hat, or spit over your right shoulder and say, 'Devil, Devil I defy thee,' or make the sign of the cross on the ground. An onion kept in the pocket gives all-day protection from single magpies. And should you see a single bird flying away from the sun, defy bad luck by throwing something after it.

BEWARE THE OWL

Though revered for its wisdom, the owl – with its nightly hooting and predatory habits – is also feared.

Owls are thought by many to be witches in disguise (and witches used parts of the birds' bodies in their 'brews'). They are especially loathed when seen flying in the daytime, and when they raise their voices. Hearing a screech owl hooting three times is thought to be a death omen. As in the cases of bats and magpies, the power of the sound can be dispelled with an appropriate action, as in this verse from the southern United States:

In Ethiopia it was an old custom that when a guilty man was condemned to death he was carried to a table on which an owl was painted. On seeing the bird he was expected to kill himself.

When you hear the screech owl,
*   honey, in the sweet gum tree,*
It's a sign as sure as you're born a death is bound
*   to be;*
Unless you put the shovel in the fire mighty quick,
For to conjure that old screech owl, take care the
*   one that's sick.*

When an owl is seen flying around the house, perching on the roof or, worst of all, flying down the chimney, the omens are bad and a family death is likely, though killing the bird may dispel bad luck. Shakespeare's Lady Macbeth hears the ominous hoot of an owl while she perpetrates her bloody deed.

OWLS AND ACTIONS

- *If you look into an owl's nest you will be unhappy for the rest of your life.*
- *An owl hoots every time a girl loses her virginity.*
- *A pregnant woman who hears an owl hoot will give birth to a girl.*
- *If you hear an owl hoot when a baby is born the child will be ill-fated.*

RESPECT THESE BIRDS

As well as being feared, birds should be treated with the greatest respect, for you never know what their real identity may be.

Larks or 'laverocks' are birds that have long been sacred. Their nests should never be molested, though it was once the custom in Germany (where the bird is protected by the Virgin Mary) to give babies roast lark as their first food to make them more pious. It is taboo to look at the nestlings with their mouths agape, revealing tongues with three black spots, each of which is said to be a curse. And do not point at one or you will get a whitlow on your finger.

> *Among the most respected of all birds are the resident ravens at the Tower of London. Legend has it that should the birds fly away the kingdom will fall.*

To avoid killing larks, the villagers of Meldreth in Cambridgeshire have, since the 13th century, paid the Earl of Clare an annual sum of three shillings in 'lark silver', in lieu of the 100 larks he demanded for his Christmas dinner.

Lapwings, said to be roaming spirits that cannot find rest, should not be touched. Even their cries sound like the words 'Bewitched, bewitched'. Swedish legend has it that the lapwing was originally the Virgin Mary's attendant, but was transformed into a bird after stealing a pair of scissors – which is why it has a scissor-shaped tail and forever cries 'Tyvit', which in Swedish means 'I stole them'.

TREAT THEM WELL
To avoid ill fortune:

• *Don't steal robin's eggs or all your fingers will grow crooked, or you might become prey to witches.*
• *Because seagulls are the souls of drowned men, you should never feed one or look it straight in the eye because, should you be swimming or in danger of drowning after a shipwreck, it will peck out your eyes.*
• *Don't kill a swallow or swift because they are 'God Almighty's gift'.*

The chirping of crickets is a sign of impending rain – and more. The 19th-century naturalist Gilbert White observed: 'They are the housewife's barometer, foretelling her when it will rain; and are prognostic sometimes, she thinks, of ill or good luck; of the death of a near relation, or the approach of an absent lover.'

FORECASTING THE WEATHER

The calls and behaviour of birds and animals were once among the country dweller's most important weather forecasters, and were taken seriously at such vital times as hay-making and harvest.

There is at least a modicum of fact to support some bird omens. In Scotland, for instance, where the frequent calling of a cuckoo is a sign of rain, it is true that episodes of poor weather – known as 'gowk storms' – coincide with the birds' arrival in spring. It is also thought that birds are sensitive to the atmospheric changes that precede rain, hence the rhymes, 'When the peacock loudly bawls/Soon we'll have both rain and squalls,' and 'If the cock goes crowing to bed/He'll certainly rise with a watery head.'

Though it may not actually rain, seeing swallows flying low means the air is damp and their insect prey are flitting near the ground. Larks fly high in the air when the weather is destined to stay fine.

BELIEVE IT IF YOU WILL

According to ancient lore, expect rain (maybe) if:

- *Asses bray.*
- *Fleas bite more than usual.*
- *Rooks sit in rows on walls or fences.*
- *A black snail crosses your path.*
- *Swans take to the air.*
- *Spiders anchor their webs with short threads.*
- *Pigs rush around with straws in their mouths.*
- *A cat washes over its ears.*

GROUNDHOG DAY AND CANDLEMAS

Predicting the arrival of spring is associated with Candlemas on 2 February, 40 days after Christmas, which is the feast of the Purification of the Virgin. In America it is Groundhog Day, when one animal's behaviour is closely observed.

The roots of Candlemas go back to at least the 6th century, when it was taken to be the middle of winter, after which the sun's intensity begins to increase. On Candlemas Eve, the feast of St Brigid, it was customary

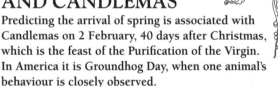

to make new effigies of the saint out of wheat or oats to ensure crop fertility (and to burn the old ones) and for a young woman to carry flowers into the home.

The bear and badger may make brief forays out of hibernation at this time, but the groundhog has been inextricably linked with Candlemas since 1886, when Clymer Freas, the editor of the *Punxsutawney Spirit* of western Pennsylvania, reported that, because the groundhog had emerged – but not seen his shadow – that day, there would be an early spring. Conversely, the emerging animal witnessing its shadow predicts another six weeks of winter. The prognosticating groundhog is often known as Punxsutawney Phil, and his predictions follow a European Candlemas tradition brought to Pennsylvania by German settlers in the 18th century. Although the groundhog's appearances are almost certainly more to do with prospecting for mates than predicting the weather, the day has retained its newsworthiness.

In the eponymous 1993 film, actor Bill Murray plays a wacky weatherman who becomes snowed in after travelling to watch the famous groundhog see his shadow and is forced to relive the same strange day over and over again until he learns the errors of his ways.

Candlemas is so named because it is the day when the church candles to be used for the rest of the year are blessed.

READING NATURE'S SIGNS

As well as Candlemas, there are other times of year when it is possible to look for a long-term weather forecast from plant as well as animal signs. Their reliability, as ever, is doubtful!

Frogs have long been used as weather forecasters. Certainly it seems logical that when, in spring, frog spawn is seen lying in deep water, then a dry spell is

predicted, while spawn at the edge of ponds and ditches means imminent rain and storms. In Europe an old tradition for predicting the weather is to keep a frog in a bowl of water and supply it with a ladder by which to climb out. As fine weather approaches the frog will ascend, and the higher it climbs the sunnier it will be. If rain is on the way, it will climb back down into its bowl.

> *Ladybirds (ladybugs) have a proven forecasting ability. In autumn, they may hide behind protective bark or leaves, in which case it will be cold, or stay out in the open on sticks and stalks – a sign of a mild winter to come.*

'Oak before ash, only a splash' is an old country prediction based on the order in which these two trees come into leaf. As the oak is almost always the first, this forecast is not really reliable, though some notably dry summers have been preceded by oak leaves opening several weeks ahead. Even less certain is a cold winter following a heavy crop of autumn berries on holly and other shrubs. This old wives' forecast is more likely to be a sign of past weather than of what is to come.

LIVING LINKS

Many weather forecasts – often in verse – have direct and indirect links with nature:

- *If there's ice in November that will bear a duck,*
The rest of the winter will be sludge and muck.
(That is, mild and wet).
- *If February brings drifts of snow*
There will be good summer crops to hoe.
- *When squirrels early start to hoard,*
Winter will pierce us like sword.
- *When in the trees the rooks build high,*
Expect the summer to be warm and dry.

AUSPICIOUS SIGNS

In the Chinese iconographic tradition, certain plants and animals have long been viewed as particularly auspicious symbols, deemed to ensure good fortune and long life.

The bamboo, renowned for the fact that it does not break in the wind, was believed to be the symbol of the upright man, steadfast in face of temptation. By similar logic, fruits such as gourds and pomegranates symbolize fertility and the birth of many children. The *lingzhi* fungus signified both longevity and immortality. The only animal able to find and eat it was the deer, which itself signifies long life.

Bats, especially when five in number, are animals of good fortune for the Chinese. This derives from their name, *fu*, which sounds like the word for 'blessings'. The blessings of the five bats are longevity, wealth, virtue, tranquillity, and a good end to life.

WORD PLAY

More Chinese ways of signifying fortune with images and puns:

Quails – an – *peace*
Goats and children playing – xiyang – *auspicious*
Chickens and roosters – ji – *good luck*
Fish – yu - *abundance*

TREES OF IMMORTALITY

Of all the world's trees the peach has some of the strongest associations with immortality, particularly in the East, where peach blossom is traditionally worn by brides.

Chinese legend relates that in her garden the Taoist goddess Xi Wang-mu, the 'Royal Mother of the West' and the personification of *yin* (the feminine element) cultivates the peach of immortality. This tree flowers only every 3000 years, and it takes another 3000 years for its fruit to ripen. When this state of perfection is achieved, Xi Wang-mu invites the immortals to eat the fruit, restoring their immortality.

Peach wood will, it is said, prolong life by warding off evil spirits and it is often used in amulets, charms and seals. As for the fruit, a peach that is oval in shape and red on one side is thought to preserve the body 'from decay until the end of the world'. At New Year, young and old alike drink peach soup to ensure longevity.

In medieval cosmology, everything was composed of the four elements, earth, air, fire and water, and each zodiacal sign was allotted to one of these. No animal signs represent air, the realm of intellect and imagination, but Aries and Leo exhibit the intensity of fire, Taurus and Capricorn share the stability of earth, and the water signs, Cancer, Scorpio and Pisces show emotion and intuition.

CREATURES OF THE ZODIAC

The creatures that feature in the zodiac relate to the constellations that bear their names. The characteristics of people born under these animal signs are believed to reflect those animals' temperaments.

The dates assigned to each sign are those when the sun is said to enter it, representing an imaginary situation in which, were the sun viewed at the same time as the constellation, its stars would be surrounding the solar orb.

Astrology, one of the oldest forms of divination, began when people tried to make links between the positions of the stars in the sky and the cycle of the seasons. Today astrology makes its predictions on the basis of the positions of certain constellations at the moment and place of a person's birth, and their conjunction with the sun, moon and planets.

The practice of astrology as we know it was begun by the Babylonians who imagined the zodiac or 'belt' in which the constellations were contained. The stars, sun and moon travelled, they believed, in three celestial 'wheels', at whose centre was the pole star.

ARIES – THE RAM

The courage and spirit of the ram are reflected in the characteristics of Arians, born between 21 March (the spring equinox) and 18 April. They are said to be idealists with implicit faith in their abilities and any causes they choose to espouse, but also to have fiery tempers.

That Aries is the first sign of the zodiac relates to the Mesopotamian myth that the world was created at the moment the sun entered this constellation. The Ram in the sky was believed to hold within it the stars of the winter solstice. It was no coincidence that in ancient Babylon the month following the spring equinox was the season in which rams, the prime symbol of the male generative force in a pastoral society, were offered as sacrifices to the gods.

Their love of domination is said to make Arians hard partners to live with and strict disciplinarians, but they excel wherever they can organize, take the lead and give rein to their intellectual powers. Their natural bent is to be guided by their instincts, though they are not noted for scheming or subtlety. Unable to be led or compelled, Arians may be easily deceived by praise or flattery – and will express their anger forcefully if find out that they have been duped.

The flowers associated with Aries are gorse, the wild rose and the thistle; trees of Aries are the holly, thorn and chestnut. The tiger and the leopard are also Arian animals.

TAURUS – THE BULL

The bull is an animal symbolic of fertility and power, associated with both the arrival of spring rains and with Zeus, king of the gods. The birth dates for Taurus are 19 April to 20 May.

It was Taurus the heavenly bull who, according to the ancient Sumerians and Babylonians, brought the vernal equinox. This was the bull created by the sky god Anu (a creature whose bellowing was said to cause thunderclaps) to confront the epic warrior hero Gilgamesh. To the Greeks, Taurus was Zeus in disguise. Appearing from the sea, he lured Europa to climb on his back and abducted her to Crete, where a bull cult became prevalent (see page 237).

Some early Christian astronomers associated Taurus with the ox which, in the Bethlehem stable, witnessed the birth of Christ.

Lily of the valley, rose, violet and myrtle are the flowers of Taurus. Lucky trees are almond, ash, apple, walnut and sycamore, and the dove is a Taurean bird of good fortune.

Taureans are lovers of beauty and nature, but no matter how vivid their flights of fancy may be they temper these with common sense. Though slow to anger, they will, when roused, display massive wrath, and they are equally tardy in forgetting slights. They shun deception and underhand dealings, naturally adopt leadership roles and revel in work that links them with the earth and with animals.

CANCER – THE CRAB

From 21 June to 22 July the sun is in the sign of Cancer, considered a 'sensitive' sign. The sign was named after the crab because, at the summer solstice (technically now in Gemini), the sun appeared to move sideways across the sky.

Astronomically, the most significant part of the constellation is a cluster of stars named the Beehive. The Chaldeans called this the Gate of Men and believed it to be the entrance taken by souls leaving heaven to take up residence in human bodies. To the Greeks, the crab was the creature that bit the feet of Heracles as he wrestled the Hydra. Though killed by the hero, the creature was rewarded by Heracles' enemy Hera (the wife of Zeus) with a place in the heavens. That the constellation appears faint, with no one bright star, is a reminder of its inauspicious end.

Poppy, water lily, willow and sycamore are lucky flowers and trees for this sign, and the owl and seagull are its birds. The otter and seal, both water-dwellers, are Cancer's lucky animals.

Like the crab, Cancereans are timid and hesitant, but tenacious. Those born under this sign are enormously sensitive, especially to criticism, and anxious over the small things in life. However they are shrewd with money (though poor gamblers) and have excellent memories. Family matters greatly to them. As befits association with a marine creature they are good sailors and happy at sea.

The Roman naturalist Pliny said that when the sun was in the sign of Cancer dead crabs lying on the sand would turn into serpents. Storms, famine and locusts were also once linked with this conjunction.

LEO – THE LION

From 23 July to 22 August the sun is in the constellation of Leo, the fifth sign of the zodiac. As positive and noble as the lion, Leos are forceful and direct, though also extremely affectionate.

One of the first astrological signs to be recognized, Leo was identified with the lion by all the major ancient civilizations and coincided, originally, with the heat of the summer solstice. In Egypt, the sun in Leo was a time when the Nile flooded, so ensuring the coming year's fertility, but it was also when lions actually appeared.

The lion has many resonances in mythology. Leo may have been the Sumerian monster Humbaba, who guarded the forest of cedars where the gods resided. It was also linked with Nergal, a god of war and pestilence commonly portrayed with a lion's body.

Simple nobility, combined with courage, are the characteristics of Leos, who are said to be strangers to fear. Their directness can make them tactless, and they can be severe in manner, even to those they love and admire. They are particularly quick to take offence if they think that their honour and dignity is being challenged in any way. Many Leos become leaders and statesmen and as such may command great devotion.

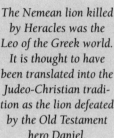

The Nemean lion killed by Heracles was the Leo of the Greek world. It is thought to have been translated into the Judeo-Christian tradition as the lion defeated by the Old Testament hero Daniel.

Yellow flowers, the colour of both sun and lion, are lucky to Leos and include marigolds, sunflowers and cowslips. The cock and the eagle are lucky birds for this sign, while trees of fortune are the palm and the laurel.

SCORPIO – THE STING IN THE TAIL

Extremes and contradictions are the outstanding attributes of Scorpios, born between 23 October and 21 November. Like the creatures whose constellation they share these humans have an infamous sting in the tail.

Orion, the giant hunter of Greek mythology, renowned for his good looks, was stung to death by Scorpio. This

The Maoris of New Zealand call the constellation of Scorpio the Fish-hook of Maui, and it is believed to have caught their islands and heaved them up from the depths of the ocean.

monster also terrified the horses of the sun when they were being driven across the heavens by Phaethon, with the result that he lost control of his chariot, which then careered across the sky scorching the Milky Way in its path. The sign is traditionally associated with cold and darkness, and even with the start of wars and other evil deeds. In ancient times the only people who relished the sun in this sign were alchemists, who believed that it was the only time when they could convert base metals into gold.

Lucky flowers and trees for Scorpios are heather and chrysanthemums, hollies and thorn trees. The wolf and the panther are Scorpio animals, and the eagle and vulture are predatory Scorpio birds.

Talented but inclined to vanity, tenacious but biting and given to tempers, Scorpios will champion the weak and oppressed, and show little regard for convention. They are ambitious – often ruthless – and remarkable achievers. They are gifted actors, whether in the theatre or merely on life's stage, but often give totally the wrong impression of their character and temperament. They are intensely loving, but can also be extraordinarily secretive and jealous.

CAPRICORN – THE GOAT

Between 22 December and 19 January, immediately following the winter solstice, the sun is in Capricorn, the sign of the goat, an animal noted for its persistence in ascending to the mountain tops.

In assessing its place in the heavens, the Chaldean astronomers of ancient Assyria assigned Capricorn to the 'Sea', a group of constellations they believed represented the army of monstrous creatures who protected Tiamat, a huge female dragon and the primordial mother. The goat was endowed with the tail of a fish, a characteristic the Greeks later explained as a result of the goat-footed god Pan being frightened by the appearance of the 'wind monster' Typhon and leaping into the water.

Capricorns are noted for being hard-working, shrewd and calculating, also reserved and often secretive. They are painstaking and methodical – stopping at nothing to achieve the goals they have set themselves – and, having supreme faith in their own abilities, are natural leaders and good communicators. By reputation they are tactful and slow to anger but equally tardy in forgetting any wrongs done to them, which can make them jealous and even vengeful.

PISCES – A FISHY DUO

The symbol of Pisces is a pair of fishes, which, though attached to each other, are moving in opposite directions, typifying those born between 19 February and 20 March.

In the heavens, the two constellations of Pisces are connected with strings of stars that look like ribbons. The Romans believed that when the love goddess Venus and the vain Cupid (who inspired her jealousy by falling in love with Psyche) were chased by Typhon they ended up in the sky. In Christian symbolism the fish are the two with which (with the five loaves) Jesus fed the multitude.

Pisceans are renowned for their dual nature. While intending to do one thing they in fact do another. With wide vision and rich imaginations they may dream up the wildest, most grandiose schemes but, when faced with reality, find themselves unable to put these into action. Romantic, kind-hearted and emotional, Pisceans are sensitive to rebuffs, though with the right guidance and backing they can achieve great things. They are also good learners and readily accumulate knowledge.

Pisces is the sign said to control the weather and, by inference, the fate of sailors. Though generally a bringer of bad luck, its links with rain made it, to early civilizations, a fertile sign.

CHINESE ASTROLOGY

Like its western equivalent, the Chinese system of astrology classifies people according to 12 signs. However, all are animal forms and the sign to which you are ascribed depends on the year (according to the Chinese calendar) in which you were born.

This ancient perspective on our modern lives comes from the ancient Oriental art of divination and character reading. Legend has it that the Buddha invited all the animals to a New Year party, but from the whole world only 12 made the effort to come. He was so touched by their attendance that he gave each the gift of a year, beginning with the party-loving rat and ending with the pig.

The day on which each year of the cycle begins is determined by the moon, so the date changes each year. Chinese New Year usually falls between 24 January and 20 February. Overlaying the 12-year cycle of animal signs there is also a 60-year cycle, linking each animal with one of five basic elements: fire, earth, metal, water and wood.

CHINESE ZODIAC ANIMAL CHARACTERS

Rat – *Ambitious, hardworking leaders, often charming to the opposite sex. Enjoy gossiping. Best with Ox, Monkey and Dragon (Years: 1936, 1948, 1960, 1972, 1984 …)*

Ox – *Responsible and hard-working, but can be bigoted, stubborn and absolutely assured they are right. Best with Rat, Snake and Rooster. (Years: 1937, 1949, 1961, 1973, 1985 …)*

Tiger – *Charismatic and courageous, deep thinkers but can be indecisive and sensitive. May be apt to show off. Best with Dog, Horse and Dragon. (Years: 1938, 1950, 1962, 1974, 1986 …)*

Rabbit (Hare) – *Financially lucky, funny, articulate, artistic and diplomatic. Peace-loving, slow to lose their tempers. Best with Dog, Goat and Bear. (Years: 1939, 1951, 1963, 1975, 1987 …)*

Dragon – *Vibrant, optimistic and brave. Inspire trust and confidence in others, but also judgmental and egotistical. Best with Rat, Snake, Rooster and Monkey. (Years: 1940, 1952, 1964, 1976, 1988 …)*

Snake – *Wise and confident, passionate but reserved, mysterious and evasive. Hate to fail. Thrifty and financially lucky. Best with Ox, Rooster and Dragon. (Years: 1941, 1953, 1965, 1977, 1989 …)*

Horse – *Talented, wise, cheerful, independent and adventurous, with many friends but slow to take advice. Best with Dog, Tiger and Goat. (Years: 1930, 1942, 1954, 1966, 1978 …)*

Goat (Ram or Sheep) – *Artistic and graceful, animated, romantic and popular, but beneath the surface may be shy, insecure and awkward. Best with Horse, Boar and Rabbit. (Years: 1931, 1943, 1955, 1967, 1979 …)*

Monkey – *Brilliant and curious, good problem solvers. Have excellent memories but can be impatient for results. Best with Rat and Dragon. (Years: 1932, 1944, 1956, 1968, 1980 …)*

Rooster – *Efficient and ambitious. Deep thinkers, but also enthusiastic, stubborn and vain with a good sense of humour. Best with Snake, Dragon and Ox. (Years: 1933, 1945, 1957, 1969, 1981 …)*

Dog – *Intensely loyal and honest, also witty and animated. A great friend, but also pessimistic and afraid of rejection, often finding fault. Best with Tiger, Rabbit and Horse. (Years: 1934, 1946, 1958, 1970, 1982 …)*

Pig (Boar) – *Generous and affectionate. Quiet, but with a thirst for knowledge and able to face life's problems head-on. Best with Goat and Rabbit. (Years: 1935, 1947, 1959, 1971, 1983 …)*

DREAMS AND PROPHECIES

Of all forms of divination, the interpretation of dreams is among the oldest. In the Bible, the Pharaoh's dream, interpreted by Joseph, was crucial to the fate of the Israelites in Egypt.

As Genesis relates, Pharaoh saw in his first dream 'seven cows, sleek and fat' followed by 'seven other cows, gaunt and lean', which devoured the seven fat animals. In his second dream he saw 'seven ears of grain, full and ripe', then after them 'seven other ears, thin and shrivelled', which swallowed up the plump ears.

> *In dreams that feature animals, their significance often relates to the character of the creature. Dreams of domestic animals are thought, in general, to mean happiness, while those of wild predators such as lions and tigers signify cruel and treacherous enemies.*

Since his own counsellors could not help him, Pharaoh sent for Joseph, who told him that the seven good cows and ears of grain represented fertile years; the thin cattle and weedy grains meant seven years of famine. He advised frugality and saving during the good years, to counter the effects of the bad. So impressed was the Pharaoh that he gave him 'authority over the whole land of Egypt'.

ANIMAL DREAMS AND THEIR MEANINGS

Elephant – *Prosperity, the arrival of new and influential friends.*

Rat – *You have powerful enemies. If you kill the rat in your dream you will defeat them.*

Fox – *Your rival or competitor. You must take immediate steps to defeat him or her.*

Dog – *Lucky if it is your own, but a strange dog is an enemy waiting to ruin you.*

Turkey – *Your actions will lead you into trouble, but the final outcome will be beneficial.*

Ass – *Be patient and good luck will come your way.*

DREAMS OF FLOWERS AND TREES

Among the many dream objects that have been subject to interpretation, flowers and trees have been linked with life and love.

Dreaming of an expanse of beautiful wild flowers may represent freedom and uninhibited growth. Conversely, the garden is a place of refuge and peace, and dreaming of one may signify happiness and even a forthcoming marriage. Some, however, interpret it as a self-imposed trap, because it is in our nature to favour safety and comfort over risk and adventure.

A dream of any tree in bud predicts new love. Luxuriant foliage denotes a happy marriage and children, but marriage problems may loom if you dream of a tree without leaves. Fruit on a tree in a dream is a sure sign of prosperity.

The meanings of flowers in dreams depend on their colour and context. Red flowers speak of romance and beauty, while white ones may symbolize purity and healing, though they are also said to foretell loss and disappointment. Beautiful, healthy flowers represent inner beauty, healthy emotions and spiritual development; dead ones the reverse. Flowers are often present in dreams about the dead, where they symbolize the natural cycle of life and death.

FLORAL REVERIE
Some more floral dream meanings:

Anemone – *Your love is untrue.*
Daffodil – *If you have fallen out with someone, seek reconciliation.*
Iris – *Expect a message bringing good news.*
Snowdrop – *confide in a friend.*

Primrose – *You will find happiness in a new friendship.*
Carnation – *Expect a passionate love affair.*
Honeysuckle – *Beware domestic quarrels.*

VISIONS OF PROSPERITY AND POVERTY

There are dozens of ways in which prosperity and general good fortune are represented in dreams that feature living things. Fruits, in particular, signify prosperity and abundance.

Of the many animals linked with money, the frog is one of the most propitious. A 19th-century *Book of Fortune* declared it to denote 'profits for the trader, good luck for the farmer, victories for the soldier and sailor and happy marriage for the lover'. The deer is seen as a bringer of good news, and is a dream symbol of both physical strength and material wealth. If you dream of a camel, expect a legacy

Dreams of birds can also be linked with money. If you are already wealthy, a dream of a bird on the wing may foretell the loss of your fortune, but if your finances are poor, dreaming of a bird in flight indicates an upward trend in your affairs. An owl in a dream may mean impending poverty while the magpie signifies a broken contract and financial misfortune.

You can also expect money to come your way if you dream of melons or figs. If you dream of apples, note their colour. Red ones are said to mean the rapid arrival of money. If they are green you will have to wait a little longer. If your desire is for great riches, golden apples are the luckiest of all.

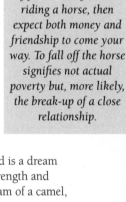

If you dream you are riding a horse, then expect both money and friendship to come your way. To fall off the horse signifies not actual poverty but, more likely, the break-up of a close relationship.

OF GODS, SPIRITS AND MONSTERS

From fire-breathing dragons to the phoenix that rises from the ashes and mermaids who lure sailors to their doom, stories abound of mythical creatures with extraordinary powers. While some of these have obvious connections with real animals and birds, others must be figments of the human imagination – though no less fascinating for that, as the continuing search for the Loch Ness monster undoubtedly proves. Perhaps we should all beware of attacks by such infamous creatures as the boggart and the bug-a-boo.

Mythology abounds with curious hybrids, like the monstrous Harpies and Gorgons, with human bodies and birds' wings. The lustful satyrs, with goats' legs but human faces, and the lascivious centaurs, which had horses' bodies, attending the god Dionysus. One look from a snake-headed Gorgon could turn a man to stone. Much more benign are the hippocampus, with a horse's head and the body of a fish, which pulled Poseidon's chariot, and the elephant-headed but one-tusked Ganesha, the Hindu god of prosperity.

Some animals and plants are thought to be people in disguise. These include werewolves – humans transformed into ravening wild animals – and vampires, the living dead who assume the form of bats. In myth, such magical transformations were often made as punishments from the gods or as ruses to confuse an enemy. Even plants like the cypress and narcissus are said to have once had a human identity, and who could resist the allure of a flower fairy?

THE MYSTERY OF MERMAIDS

Many legends tell of creatures – half woman, half fish – that inhabit the seas. It is widely believed to be unlucky to see one – and even worse to kill one. They are said to be able to predict storms. Grasping the belt or cap of a mermaid will give a mortal power over her.

Mermaids, so it is said, live beneath the sea in a land of riches and splendour. From here they lure seafarers to their deaths, then gather up the souls of the dead and keep them in cages. 'The Mermaid', one of a collection of traditional songs assembled by FrancisJames Child in the 19th century, relates how:

In Irish lore, mermaids are called merrows. They are old, pagan women who foretell bad weather, banished from the earth by St Patrick. It is said that the coastal region of Machaire is inhabited by people descended from the union of a man and a mermaid.

'True life' mermaids are probably dugongs or manatees, rare marine mammals with heads that somewhat resemble humans in profile and fish-shaped tails. While suckling their single young the females cradle the babies to their breasts with one flipper, in the manner of human mothers.

> *'Twas Friday morn when we set sail,*
> *And we had not got far from land,*
> *When the Captain, he spied a lovely mermaid,*
> *With a comb and a glass in her hand.*

In the final verse the ballad tells of the disaster that befalls following the sighting:

> *Then three times 'round went our gallant ship,*
> *And three times 'round went she,*
> *And the third time that she went 'round*
> *She sank to the bottom of the sea.*

In Hans Christian Andersen's tale, 'The Little Mermaid', the sea creature falls in love with a prince in a passing ship. In order to be with him, she asks a sea witch to give her human form but has to pay for it with her tongue and is doomed to perpetual silence. Although she waits on him assiduously, he marries a 'true' human. Her heart is broken. Though she is given the chance to regain her mermaid's tail by killing the prince, she kills herself instead and joins the 'daughters of the air', spirits destined to wait 300 years for immortality.

FAIRY RINGS AND FAIRY FLOWERS

Many plants have links with fairies, but the grassy green 'fairy rings' of damp autumnal lawns and fields are especially associated with them.

Fairy rings (circles of rich, deep green grass that are in fact produced by the activity of fungi spreading outward and releasing nutrients in the soil) are special places that humans interfere with at their peril. Said to be fairies' dancing places, it is deemed unwise to step inside them. In some places it is believed that, with the help of the fairies, treasure has been buried in the centre of the ring.

The fairies' tree:
Fairies were believed to meet under a single hawthorn (Crataegus monogyna), *called a lone or fairy thorn. Such trees were to be avoided at all costs. Both fairies and witches were thought to be especially active on May Day, of which hawthorn or May blossom is the emblem.*

The Flower Fairies, *a series of books illustrated with charming portraits of children dressed in floral or leafy garb, each with an accompanying botanical poem, were the work of the English artist Cicely Mary Barker, born in 1895. Still hugely popular worldwide, their number includes the Crocus Fairies, 'Each with a flame in its shining cup' who dance for joy '… and sing/The song of the coming again of Spring.'*

Ragwort (*Senecio squalidus*), a plant fatal to horses if they eat it, was thought to be a plant on which fairies rode around the world doing mischief. To stop them entering a byre – and harming cattle – holy pearlwort (*Sagina procumbens*) was placed over the door. This is said to be the first plant Jesus stepped on when he rose from the dead. The same plant was placed below the right knee of a woman while she was in labour to keep the fairies away from her when she and her baby were at their most vulnerable.

PHOENIX RISING

The ancient symbol of the sun (which reappeared each morning) and later of the Resurrection, the phoenix is a bird whose legend has been hugely embellished over the centuries.

The phoenix legend may have arisen from the vulture's habit of taking and flying off with burning pieces of flesh from funeral pyres.

According to a well-known version of its myth, the phoenix, said to live for 500 years, is a male bird with beautiful plumage that lives in Arabia. At the end of its life cycle it builds itself a nest of cassia and frankincense twigs, on which it sits to sing a song of rare beauty. The nest is then set on fire by the sun's rays. Both nest and bird burn fiercely and are reduced to ashes. Out of the ashes of the dead phoenix crawls a worm, and from this a new, young phoenix arises. The new phoenix embalms the ashes of the old one in an egg made of myrrh, which it takes to Heliopolis (the Egyptian city of the sun) where it buries the parent bird in the temple before returning to Arabia.

The phoenix was the badge of Jane Seymour, the beloved third wife of Henry VIII. It was also a favourite device of Queen Elizabeth I because it symbolized sacrifice and renewal.

The Roman naturalist Pliny described the phoenix as being '… as big as an eagle, in colour yellow, and bright as gold, namely all about the neck, the rest of the body a deep red purple; the tail azure blue, intermingled with feathers among of rose carnation colour …'

A Persian creature similar to the phoenix is the fabulous Simurgh (see page 242). According to one legend it lives for up to 1700 years, and when the young bird hatches the parent of the opposite sex burns itself to death.

HIDEOUS WINGED MONSTERS

Among the most fearsome creatures of mythology are those with bird-like wings, including the ghastly Harpies and the Gorgons. Their evil powers, especially their calls, were able to wreck the lives of humans.

The head of Medusa is an ancient icon used on shields and breastplates to protect warriors against slaughter.

The Harpies were monsters with the heads of women but the claws and wings of eagles or vultures, and were loathsome to behold. Personifications of the storm winds, they were robbers, who carried people off to be tormented in the underworld. Their names forcefully reflect the strength of their malign influence: Aello means 'storm'; Celaeno 'blackness' and Ocypete 'rapid'. They were portrayed on Greek monuments as symbols of death.

The word 'harpy' is now used of a greedy, predatory woman, while a gorgon is a woman renowned for the strength of her temper.

Notorious for their hair of living serpents, the three hideous Gorgons were endowed with golden wings and bronze claws. Just one look from them could turn an unfortunate human to stone. The Greek poet Hesiod includes in their number the queen Medusa, the only mortal of the trio. In legend, Medusa met her end when her head was struck off by the hero Perseus, who avoided her lethal gaze by using the polished shield of Athene as a mirror to look at her as he wielded his sword. Afterwards, Athene set the head with its writhing snakes in the centre of her shield.

THE ELUSIVE SEA SERPENTS

Though their existence – and their identity – is disputed, sightings of sea serpents have been regularly reported since ancient times, and they have been held responsible for the fatal wrecking of ships.

No creature consistent with descriptions of a sea serpent has ever been washed ashore. Decaying remains of basking sharks have been put forward as possibilities, but the mystery remains. Perhaps, some speculate, this is because the sea serpent confines itself to deep water. Whether it is a relation of the giant squid (or the Kraken) or an eel, shark or turtle, is yet to be determined.

'Among fishermen with long experience,' said Aristotle, 'some claim to have to have seen in the sea animals like beams of wood, black, round and the same thickness throughout.' To others they appeared to have flowing manes like horses; yet others noticed long heads and scaly skins like those of crocodiles.

One vivid report of an undulating, snake-like creature seen off Gloucester Bay, Massachusetts, in 1817 reads: 'We counted twenty bunches [humps] … His head was of a dark brown colour, formed like a seal's and shined with a glossy appearance … his head was large as a barrel for we could see it when he was about four miles from us.'

As well as more than 400 seemingly bona fide sightings there have been many hoaxes. These include the 1871 description of a beast with '... an enormous fan-shaped tail ... overlapping scales [which] ... open and shut with every arch of his sinuous back coloured like a rainbow ...'

SEA SERPENT TRAITS

Features consistently reported down the years include:

- *Many small humps along the back.*
- *Several big coils visible above the water.*
- *A mane on the neck.*
- *Prominent eyes.*
- *A long neck and small head.*
- *Many fins.*

NORWAY'S OWN KRAKEN

On hot days, so Norwegian sailors of the 16th century reported, the sea would turn murky and the monstrous Kraken would emerge. When it sank again, it created a great whirlpool that could pull the largest ship to its doom.

The bonus of this risky situation for the fishermen was that the appearance of the Kraken coincided with an abundance of fish. What also happened was that the sea suddenly decreased in depth – a signal they took to mean that the animal was about to surface. This recalls the phenomenon of the 'deep scattering layer' of myriad small squid, which causes echo-sounders to give false readings. And the Kraken itself was almost certainly a

In his 1953 sci-fi novel The Kraken Wakes, *John Wyndham tells the story of a world in which the seas are occupied by a foreign life form that has arrived from outer space in an attempt to take over the earth. Its American title was* Out of the Deeps.

giant squid. First described by Erik Pontoppidan in his 1752 *History of Norway*, the Kraken lives on in Norwegian legend. A bishop was even said to have celebrated a mass on its back, taking it to be an island. In his *Juvenilia*, published when he was 21, Tennyson included a poem dedicated to this sea monster.

> Below the thunders of the upper deep,
> Far, far beneath the abysmal sea,
> His ancient, dreamless, uninvaded sleep
> The Kraken sleepeth: faintest sunlights flee
> About his shadowy sides; above him swell
> Huge sponges of millennial growth and height;
> And far away into the sickly light,
> From many a wondrous grot and secret cell
> Unnumber'd and enormous polypi
> Winnow with giant arms the slumbering green.
> There he hath lain for ages, and will lie
> Battening upon huge sea-worms in his sleep,
> Until the latter fire shall heat the deep;
> Then once by man and angels to be seen,
> In roaring he shall rise and on the surface die.

THE MONSTER OF THE LOCH

Most famed of all the unidentified water dwellers is Scotland's Loch Ness Monster. The subject of media hype and hoaxes, as well as serious scientific investigation, 'Nessie's' true identity remains a mystery.

Reports of a creature in Loch Ness go back at least 1500 years. St Adomnan's medieval *Life of St Columba* tells how, in 565 CE, Columba, by raising his voice to the creature, saved the life of a Pict who was being attacked by it in the river Ness. On 2 May 1933, the

Inverness Courier (whose editor dubbed the creature 'a monster') ran the story of Mr and Mrs John Mackay, who had seen 'an enormous animal rolling and plunging' on the surface of Loch Ness. In the media frenzy that ensued, a circus offered a reward of £20,000 for the monster's capture.

Reports of Nessie have continued to flow ever since this incident. In March 1994, however, it came to light that one Marmaduke Wetherell had faked the famous photograph of a long-necked creature that was attributed to surgeon RK Wilson in 1934. In another hoax, the ornithologist Sir Peter Scott named the creature *Nessiteras rhombopteryx* after seeing a blurred underwater photograph taken in the early 1970s by a group led by the American lawyer Robert Rines. The name is an anagram of 'monster hoax by Sir Peter S'.

Various theories have been proposed for the monster's identity. These include a pre-historic plesiosaur and the species of sturgeon that has been found in streams close to Loch Ness. Another theory is that the 'humps' are in fact disruptions of the water caused by minor volcanic activity at the bottom of the Loch.

THE CULT OF NESSIE

The Loch Ness Monster has appeared in many fictional – often bizarre – contexts.

Doctor Who – *In the 1975 series, it is an alien cyborg controlled by extraterrestrial Zygons.*

The Simpsons – *In episode 224, 'Monty Can't Buy Me Love', Mr Burns, Homer and others drain the loch, capture the monster and take it back to the USA. Mr Burns gives it a job in a casino.*

Freddie as FR07 – *Jon Acevski's 1992 animated parody of the Bond films, in* which Scottie the monster befriends an enchanted frog prince, and together they defeat an enemy wreaking revenge on the world by shrinking landmarks all over London.

The Private Life of Sherlock Holmes – *Billy Wilder's 1970 classic in which Holmes encounters the monster while investigating a secret society who are developing a submarine in the Loch.*

MYSTIC WATER HORSES

Among the weird inhabitants of the water are horse-like creatures with mystical powers that may get up to mischief.

Hippocampus is the generic name of the sea horse, an oddity of the fish world, which has a horse-like head and swims upright. It is also peculiar in that the male 'gives birth' to the young. When the fish mate the female lays her eggs in the 'brood pouch' on his belly. Because it looks rather like a sea horse, an area of the brain is named the hippocampus. Lying in the 'primitive', unconscious part of the brain, it is involved with the processing of memories.

The chariot of the Greek sea god Poseidon was pulled by a hippocampus, whose name comes from *hippos*, a horse, and *kampos*, a sea monster. It had a horse's head and upper body and hind parts like a fish or dolphin. As Poseidon rode through the waters the waves opened ahead of him so that his chariot did not get wet and sea monsters swam up from the depths to pay him homage.

By contrast, mischief-making was the penchant of the Kelpie, a water-horse of Gaelic folklore similar to the Icelandic Nykur. This creature, with backward pointing hooves, could change its shape at will. It led men astray by enticing them to ride it across a river, then plunged into the water and drowned them. Disaster was most likely to strike if the rider mentioned Christ's name.

FOLLOW THE FOOTPRINTS

Some of the world's most elusive creatures – if they exist at all – are known only from the footprints they are alleged to leave. These have given rise to legends such as those of Bigfoot and the Jersey Devil.

Bigfoot, a huge ape-like creature believed to tramp across various parts of north-western USA and western Canada, was 'discovered' in 1811 by the British explorer

David Thompson. Its footprints have supposedly been measured at 2ft (60cm) long and 8in (20cm) wide. Despite a convincing film made in 1967, its existence is yet to be confirmed.

The Yeti, also dubbed 'the Abominable Snowman', roams (if it does exist) the Himalayas where, to the Nepalese, it is significant as a spiritual rather than an actual physical entity. Said to be ape-like, 10ft (3m) tall, with feet twice the size of a man's, its footprints are believed to range over vast tracts of open snow. In reality, these may well be the prints of human boots enlarged by the melting of the snow.

In 1735, a Mrs Leeds in New Jersey was said to have given birth to a cursed child (her 13th) with a horse's head and hooves, wings and a snake's tail. During the 19th century this being was seen from time to time, but over a five-day period in January 1909 over 100 people reported sightings. As well as hoof prints in the snow, there were accounts of the Jersey Devil flying over towns and attacking domestic animals.

The Chupacabra, an alleged predator of South America whose name is Spanish for 'goat sucker', is said to drink the blood of various farm animals, leaving their corpses in the fields with incision wounds on their necks. Some people claim to have seen the creature in remote areas, and it is often described as having 'spines' down its back.

The study and research of new and undiscovered species of animals is known as cryptozoology.

TALES OF THE THUNDERBIRD

By flapping its wings it caused thunderclaps to roar. As it blinked, lightning flashed in the sky. So runs the story of the gigantic thunderbird of North American Indian folklore.

There is more. The bird's hollow back was said to hold a reservoir of water that could be released as a deluge of rain. It was so strong that it could carry a whale in its claws, killed with arrows fired from its wings.

The bones of the whale were left on the mountain tops. Some tribes believe that trees destroyed in storms have been ripped open by the thunderbird's claws to extract the huge grubs that are its favourite food.

As well as influencing the weather, in the mythology of Plains and Woodlands Indians the thunderbird wages constant warfare with underwater creatures, especially horned snakes. Northwest Indians, who depict the thunderbird on their tepees, are among those for whom the images are a means of warding off the attentions of evil spirits.

Thunderbirds, first aired in 1965, was a children's action-adventure TV show set in the 2020s. Made by Sylvia and Gerry Anderson, it used a new form of puppetry they called 'Supermarionation'. The show's title came from a letter written to his family by Gerry Anderson's older brother during World War II, while he was serving on an American airbase called 'Thunderbird Field'.

In some American tales, thunder is the rattle of a black rattlesnake, which carries a supernatural creature on its back. For others it is the sound of a great bat's wing.

THE EARTH SHAKERS

In their attempt to explain violent natural events such as earthquakes, the ancients held all kinds of creatures to be responsible, from fish to serpents.

When he shakes one of his thousand heads, so Hindu myth relates, Sesha, the world serpent, makes earthquakes occur. His power comes from the fact that he supports the earth, and he is also said to destroy it with fire every 1000 years. Traditionally represented dressed in purple and holding a plough and a pestle, he acts as the resting place for Vishnu, the solar deity. In Japanese tradition, Jinshin Uwo, the earthquake fish, is the creature upon which the islands of Japan float. As the creature lashes its tail, it causes the tremors that characterize earthquakes.

According to the Dahomey of West Africa, the rainbow serpent Aido Hwedo helped to create the universe by transporting the god Mawu through the cosmos. Aido Hwedo also created the mountains, which were said to be his excrement. However, the earth became far too heavy, so the god ordered the serpent to coil beneath the world to hold it up. Because Aido Hwedo could not bear the heat, Mawu created the sea to surround and cool him. If he gets uncomfortable and shifts his position, earthquakes occur. In order to remain strong, Aido Hwedo needs to consume a large number of iron bars. When the supply of these runs out, it is said, Aido Hwedo will eat his own tail, making the world fall into the sea.

The time of day at which an earthquake occurs can add to the woes it may bring, and affect the weather, as this old rhyme relates:
'These are things
An earthquake brings:
At nine of the bell
They sickness foretell;
At five and seven they
betoken rain;
At four the sky is
cleared thereby;
At six and eight comes
wind again.'

THE BREATH OF VOLCANIC GIANTS

When Mount Etna erupts, shooting fire into the Sicilian sky, the monster Typhon is at work. Other creatures have also been believed since ancient times to be the mighty forces responsible for nature's rage.

The giant Typhon, hybrid of man and beast and taller than any mountain, was endowed with a coiled viper's tail, wings and feathers. The offspring of the earth goddess Gaia, his most fearsome feature was his 100 dragon heads, with their dark tongues, fiery eyes and thunderous voices.

Greek legend relates that as soon as Typhon had emerged from the cave in which he was born he was attacked by Zeus with a hail of thunderbolts. But instead of hiding himself away, Typhon attacked the king of the gods, leaving him helpless on the ground – minus the sinews in his limbs. Zeus, however, had his revenge. With his sinews restored he finally conquered Typhon by tearing off a piece of Italy and using it to crush the monster. Typhon's breath (he lives on because he is immortal) is the evidence of his presence, still erupting from Mount Etna.

Alcyoneus, a huge ass whose name means 'the brayer', was supposedly a manifestation of the Mediterranean wind, the Sirocco. This destructive monster was one of the Gigantes, a race of giants.

The typhoon or tropical cyclone – formed by colliding masses of air – gets its name not only from the Greek *tuphon*, meaning whirlwind, but also from the Chinese *tai fung* meaning 'great wind'.

CURSES OF THE 'WERE' CREATURES

Werewolves – humans able to turn themselves at will into ravening wild animals – have been feared since real wolves roamed at large among our ancestors' habitations. These embodiments of evil are based on the concept of the 'the beast within'.

Influenced by the mysterious process known as lycanthropy, witches, sorcerers and others with evil powers were believed able to turn themselves into wolves. (The term 'werewolf' comes from the Old English word *wer*, meaning man.) The 19th-century author Emma Phipson vividly conjures their menace: 'Human beings when under this delusion,' she says, 'roamed through forests and desert places actuated by the same passions as the wild beasts whose name they bore. They howled, walked on all fours, tore up graves in search of prey, attacked unarmed passengers, devoured children, and committed the wildest excesses.'

In the 2005 movie hit from animator Nick Park, Wallace and Gromit go on the trail of a were-rabbit, which is eating prize-winning vegetables.

Where fear of werewolves took hold it could cause panic in entire communities. It is reported that in 1600, in the Jura mountains between France and Switzerland, lycanthropy was so rife that men and women gathered themselves into packs and roamed the country. And in France, the *loup-garou* is still an object of terror. No weapon is effective against a werewolf unless, some believe, it has been blessed in a chapel dedicated to St Hubert, the patron saint of hunters (see page 52).

Apart from wolves, other 'were' creatures are known in various parts of the world. In South America, for instance, there is a persistent belief in were-jaguars.

The concept of the werewolf resonates strongly in legends surrounding Lycaon, the mythical ruler of Arcadia. In the most common, related by Ovid, Lycaon was turned into a wolf because he angered Zeus by serving him a 'hash of human flesh' when the god visited Lycaon's court in the guise of a simple traveller; this was a child sacrifice, possibly of Lycaon's own son. This gave rise to the story that a man was turned into a wolf at each annual sacrifice to Zeus, but recovered his human form if he abstained from human flesh for ten years.

TALES OF THE VAMPIRE

Though anyone who sucks blood is called a vampire, in the natural world it is vampire bats that have the most bloodthirsty reputation. But most fearsome are the 'living dead' – the vampires who, often in bat form, attack unwary innocents.

Of all supernatural monsters the vampire is among the best known. Traditionally, his eyes gleam red, his breath is foul, his fingernails pointed and he has hairs on the palms of his hands. Some are said to have only a single nostril. Returning from the grave, complete with bats' wings, the vampire is said to turn his victim into yet another such horror with his bite.

The idea existed in legend long before Bram Stoker crystallized it into Dracula, taking the monster's name from *dracul*, the Romanian word for 'devil'. Where vampire activity was believed to be rife, it was customary to take a white stallion that had never been to stud – and never stumbled – into a graveyard. Any graves that the horse refused to walk over were those of vampires.

A force for good: *the American Stroke Association has reported the success of a drug made from the saliva of the vampire bat in busting the clots that lodge in the brain and cause strokes.*

AGAINST A VAMPIRE

To defend yourself against a vampire it is said that you should:

- Wear a silver amulet, or carry any silver object in your pocket.
- Wear garlic flowers around your neck or place them in the window – vampires hate their smell.
- Carry or wear a crucifix – the symbol of Christ will neutralize the evil.

And to destroy a vampire …
- Drive a stake through its heart.
- Or shoot it with a silver bullet, ideally made from a crucifix that has been melted down.

THE CROAK OF THE EVIL TOAD

Toads are feared as witches or evil men in animal form, although 'toad-magic' is also an old means of destroying witches' powers.

At the trial of the Bury St Edmunds witches in 1665, a Dr Jacob declared that he had found a toad in the bed of a child named Amy Duny. After he had thrown the creature in the fire, Amy developed burns on her arms – a sure sign of a witch acting in disguise.

The natural reaction of a toad, when alarmed, to exude various poisonous irritants is undoubtedly significant to its links with witchcraft.

Toadmen, able to make the most unruly horse stand still, were recorded in England. To acquire such powers a man had to skin a toad or peg it to an anthill until the insects had stripped its bones clean. He then had to carry the bones in his pocket until they were dry and, at midnight under a full moon, float them on a stream. The bones would screech and one would detach itself and head upstream. Catching this 'rogue' bone bestowed a toadman's powers.

ANTI-WITCH TREATMENT

Toads were used in this charm to rob a witch of her evil attributes, and prevent her from influencing your life.

1 *Take three small-necked jars.*
2 *Place in each a toad's heart studded with thorns and a frog's liver into which new pins have been inserted.*
3 *Cork the jars and bury them in three different churchyards, 7in (17.5cm) below the surface and 7ft (2.1m) from the church porch.*
4 *During each burial, say the Lord's Prayer backwards.*

BEWARE THE BASILISK'S GLANCE

A small serpent with a deadly glance, the basilisk or cockatrice also had venomous breath. Humans, animals, birds and plants were all prey to its deadly habits.

The mirror was the perfect protection and weapon against a basilisk. If seen in a mirror, rather than in the flesh, it became harmless. And if it looked at its own reflection it died of terror.

Even if it had no intent to kill, just one look from the basilisk could be fatal. Because it slew everything in sight, this fabulous creature was believed to live in a desert of its own creation. It had, according to the Roman naturalist Pliny, a whitish, crown-like marking on its head, which led to its being dubbed the 'king of all serpents'. Most accounts agree that it had the head and body of a cockerel and a serpent's tail, though the horrible aspects of its appearance were embroidered over the centuries so that by the Middle Ages it had become a four-legged cock with a crown on its head, yellow feathers, thorny wings and a serpent's tail armed with either a hook or another cock's head.

Real basilisks are lizards native to South America. Because they can run across the surface of water they are also known as Jesus lizards.

It was widely believed that basilisks hatched from cockerel's eggs, ideally laid in dunghills or amidst poisonous materials of some kind, and incubated by a toad or a serpent. When such tales were beginning to be challenged by science, the Spanish satirist and poet Quevedo, in his romance *The Basilisk*, wrote of this creature: 'If the man who saw you is still alive, your whole story is a lie, since if he has not died he cannot have seen you, and if he has died, he cannot tell what he saw.'

GIANT CREATURES, FEARSOME REPUTATIONS

On land and sea – and in the underworld – huge creatures lie in wait to do damage to the sinful and unwary. So mythology relates, and the theme has been adopted in modern times, notably in such classic movies as *King Kong*.

The eponymous screen giant King Kong, star of the 1933 movie (and various remakes since, the latest in 2005), is an altogether more touching creature. When brought to New York as a circus attraction from Skull Island in the Indian Ocean, he runs amok and climbs the Empire State building, gently carrying the young woman he loves. His pathetic end comes when fighter planes gun him down.

When they cast their spells, the cabalists, practitioners of the ancient secret lore, deem as most powerful the one used to summon up Leviathan, the great fish. This fearsome beast, a monster of the deep, is described in the Book of Job: 'Out of his mouth go burning lamps, and sparks of fire leap out … He maketh the deep [sea] boil like a pot.' So evil is the beast that only on the Day of Judgment will he meet his end when 'his flesh will be food for the righteous'.

Guarding the Egyptian underworld was Ammut, part hippopotamus and part lion, with the jaws of a crocodile. Specifically stationed next to the scales of judgment in the hall of Osiris (the king and judge of the dead) she ate the hearts of those who were burdened with sin. Her role was similar to that of the Greek Cerberus, the three-headed dog who guarded the gates of Hades.

'Giants' can take many forms. Ethiopian ants as large as dogs were described by the Latin scholar Solinus as being particularly skilled in digging for gold. Any human who tried to steal from their precious hoard was devoured on sight. Similar creatures were also reputed to exist in India.

THE SERPENT GOD

Known throughout Middle America, the serpent god Quetzalcoatl (whose name means 'green feather snake') was originally the god of the air and wind but was also a divine creator and the ruler of the ancient Toltec people.

Quetzalcoatl is, at once, heaven and earth, light and darkness, life and death. As a creator god he travelled to Mictlan, the underworld, retrieved some bones and sprinkled them with his blood, bringing human life into being. He was also a teacher, showing people how to farm and weave cotton and also how to make calendars and interpret the movements of the stars.

According to Toltec myth, a pale skinned god-king named Quetzalcoatl was sent into exile by the dark god Tezcatlipoca ('smoking mirror'), and crossed the Gulf of Mexico on a raft of snakes, vowing to return. When, in 1519 (considered an auspicious year by the Aztecs, who claimed descent from the Toltecs) the Spanish adventurer Hernán Cortés – a pale-skinned European – arrived on the coast of Mexico he was believed to be the returning god. As a result, the Aztec emperor Montezuma received Cortés graciously, but was captured and killed during the Spanish conquest of the Aztec capital.

The resplendent quetzal (Pharomachrus mocinno) is a spectacular resident of the forests to the east of the Bolivian Andes, its red front contrasting starkly with its metallic green back, white undertail and long shimmering green tail feathers. To the ancient Maya the quetzal symbolized freedom – because a quetzal will die in captivity – and wealth, because quetzal feathers were, with jade, the Maya traders' most sought-after treasures.

The plumes on the head of Quetzalcoatl are those of the quetzal bird, a creature still celebrated in Mexican festival dances. Dressed in sumptuous feathered costumes, the dancers, called quetzales, *perform a set of ritual steps that scholars think is a tribute to the life-giving powers of the sun.*

FEARSOME CRITTERS

This is the folklorists' title for a collection of outlandish mythical creatures, many with wonderful names like Giddyfish and Teakettlers, that it is supposedly possible to encounter in the American backwoods.

The lumberjacks and frontiersmen of old amused themselves by telling tall stories concerning bizarre creatures. Typical was the Hoop Snake, 'invented' in the 19th century, which put its tail in its mouth and bowled over the ground at a rate of knots. The only way a person could escape it was to jump through the hoop, which made the serpent so confused that it was unable to turn back.

BIZARRE ZOOLOGY

Some of the more outrageous fearsome critters:

Giddyfish – *Fish with elastic bodies. In winter, when one emerged from a hole in the ice it had to be hit on the head with a paddle. This made it bounce up and down; then all the others would do the same and jettison themselves on to land.*

Rumptifusel – *A furry but belligerent creature that slept wrapped around a tree trunk. Lumberjacks mistaking it for a fur coat were attacked and killed.*

Gillygaloo – *A bird that laid cuboid eggs because it nested on hills. When hard-boiled, they could be used as dice.*

Teakettler – *A small animal that walked backwards while ejecting clouds of steam from its nostrils and making a noise like a boiling kettle.*

Goofus – *A bird that flew backwards because it was interested only in places it had already visited. It also built its nest upside down.*

Squonk – *An unhappy, shy creature with skin covered in warts and moles that could be tracked by the trail of tears it left as it moved. If frightened, its body dissolved, leaving only a puddle.*

THE UNICORN – ONE-HORNED WONDER

Of all legendary beasts, the unicorn is among the most famous, and appears on the royal coat of arms of the United Kingdom. It is widely regarded as a symbol of purity, and as such is associated with the Virgin Mary.

Because of its meekness, the unicorn was believed, in medieval times, to be the animal that would inherit the earth, a reference to the words of the Bible.

'The fiercest animal,' wrote Pliny, 'is the unicorn, which in the rest of the body resembles a horse, but in the head a stag, in the feet an elephant, and in the tail a boar, and has a deep bellow, and a single black horn three feet long projecting from the middle of the forehead. They say that it is impossible to capture this animal alive.'

The unicorn's horn was endowed with magical and medicinal properties, according to the Greek physician Ctesias in the 4th century BC. Dust filed from it was an antidote to all poisons and 'deadly drugs', and it would purify the water in a well, especially if used to trace the sign of the cross. Horns reputed to have such powers, probably the tusks of narwhals, were prized in the courts of Renaissance Europe.

The horn of the unicorn was once used to detect the presence of poison in the food of kings. Just a single touch, it was said, was sufficient to reveal a life-threatening ingredient.

THE UNICORN'S FRIENDS AND FOES

Although fierce, the unicorn was believed to love purity – and so could be tamed by a virgin. Symbolically its greatest enemy was the lion.

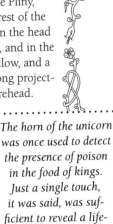

The Greek *Physiologus* was specific in its instructions. In the text headed 'How it is captured', the advice ran thus:

'A virgin is placed before it and it springs into the virgin's lap and she warms it with love and carries it off to the palace of kings.' The unicorn's undoing, according to Leonardo da Vinci, was its lust, which made it forget to be fierce. Whatever the truth, the unicorn became a symbol of chastity – of both men and women – because only a pure woman could tame the 'horn' of male desire.

The capture of the unicorn, for which a beautiful, naked virgin had to be tied to a tree in order to attract the beast, may have been based on a trick used by Indian hunters in which they used a monkey to lure a rhinoceros, which could then be captured. It became the allegory of the Holy Hunt, in which Christ is the unicorn who is attracted by the Virgin Mary and killed to save the world's sinners.

> *In Christian art that depicts both the unicorn and the Virgin Mary the horn is said by scholars to symbolize the penetration of her body by the Holy Spirit. In secular representations of scenes from mythology the female embodiment of chastity is often depicted riding in a chariot pulled by unicorns.*

THE LION AND THE UNICORN

The contest between these two great beasts is thought to symbolize the triumph of summer over spring, and can be traced back to at least 3500 BC. The nursery rhyme written in the early 18th century probably refers to the amalgamation of the arms of Scotland with those of England following the accession of James I (James VI of Scotland) in 1603.

The lion and the unicorn
Were fighting for the crown;
The lion beat the unicorn
All around the town.

Some gave them white bread,
And some gave them brown;
Some gave them plum cake
And drummed them out of town.

'HERE BE DRAGONS'

… Or so it was written on outlines of remote parts of the world by early mapmakers. Dragons bad and good feature in myth and legend all over the world.

With the head and horns of a ram, a lion's forelimbs, a scaly reptilian body (like that of a crocodile) and an eagle's claws, the dragon depicted in white glaze on the Ishtar Gate in ancient Babylon is one of the oldest known renditions of this mythical creature. From it evolved the familiar fearsome animal with sharp talons, forked tongue, glaring eyes (often glowing with a red reflection from the treasures it guarded), flared nostrils breathing fire capable of destroying anything in its path – even entire countries – and a thunderous voice.

Dragoons were originally mounted infantrymen, so called because in the 18th century they used weapons called 'dragons'. These carbines got their name from the burst of flame they produced when fired.

Dragons of old were so omnipotent that they could control not only the weather – bringing about eclipses by swallowing the sun or moon – but also the destiny of humankind. In many cultures dead men were thought to become dragons, and there was also a belief that after death the souls of the wicked would be left to the mercy of a fire-breathing dragon. When the dead were buried with their earthly treasures, it was dragons who guarded this bounty. Another belief was that, if planted, dragons' teeth would grow into an army of men.

As a symbol of power, the dragon was adopted by the Romans as an icon on their standard, and it is the association with invading Romans that is thought to have led King Henry VII, who was of Welsh descent, to use it on his coat of arms.

The Greek word *drakos*, meaning 'eye', is the root of the dragon's name, and ties in with the idea that the dragon is a guardian of treasure. In the Christian tradition, however, it is often interchangeable with the serpent. So in Revelation, in St Michael's battle, 'the great dragon was thrown down, that ancient serpent that was called the Devil …'

DRAGON LANGUAGE

Many current words and phrases maintain a link with the mythological beast, including:

To chase the dragon – *to smoke opium or heroin. The fumes produced look like dragons' breath.*

Flying dragon – *a colloquial term for a meteor.*

To sow dragon's teeth – *to do something intended to quell strife, but which in fact foments it even more.*

Dragon's blood – *a reddish-brown resin with a spicy fragrance extracted from palms such as Calamus draco. Jilted lovers traditionally throw it on the fire and chant a rhyme in order to restore their broken dreams.*

Dragon's teeth – *anti-tank obstacles used in World War II.*

THE DRAGON CONQUERORS

Heroes of old, both saints and knights, made their reputations by fighting and killing dragons, thus symbolizing the triumph of good over evil.

Of all the dragon conquerors St George is the exemplar. Having battled victoriously against the Saracens, so the story goes, he travelled to Libya where a dragon was terrorizing the local population and demanding a virgin every day. Sabra, the king's daughter, was about to be sacrificed to the monster when St George arrived on his white charger. Having fought

In Mesopotamian myth, the heavens and the earth were created when the dragon Tiamat was killed by the king of the gods.

and wounded the dragon he attached it to Sabra's girdle; she led it into the city where the citizens disposed of it.

In days when knights were bold it was a supreme act of chivalry – indeed the only means of achieving the highest rank – to slay a dragon. A 17th-century ballad, *The Dragon of Wantley*, parodied the many medieval romances that described their gallantry to tell the story of a heroic lawyer who challenged the church's excessive demands for tithes in Wharncliffe, near Sheffield. In it, Sir More of More Hall (the lawyer) takes on the task of fighting the dragon of Wantley (Wharncliffe), which has been killing cattle and devouring forests and even houses. His promised reward is a 16-year-old maiden with a lovely smile and 'hair as black as a sloe'. The anonymous poet paints a vivid picture of his foe:

How St George became England's patron saint is a mystery. In the 12th century, the crusaders were probably the first to call for his help in battle, but his position was most likely secured in 1350 when Edward III founded the Order of the Garter in his name.

This dragon had two furious wings
Each one upon each shoulder,
With a sting in his tail as long as a flail,
Which made him bolder and bolder,
He had long claws, and in his jaws,
Four and forty teeth of iron …'

ENTER THE DRAGON

Essentially benign, unlike their western counterparts, the dragons of the East were believed to control different aspects of the world. Their ancient powers are remembered in the dragon dances that still take place at Chinese New Year.

Wang Fu, a Chinese philosopher of the Han Dynasty (206 BC – 220 AD) painted a vivid portrait of the eastern dragon. It had a complex make up – a camel's head with stag's horns, an elephant's tusks, demon's eyes and cow's ears. Its triple-jointed body, ending in a serpent's tail, had a clam's belly, a carp's scales, an eagle's claws and the feet of a tiger. Of the creature's 117 scales, he said, 81 are imbued with yang, and 36 with yin, making its good influences outweigh the bad, and ensuring that it is essentially male, rather than female.

To the ancients, the most important role of eastern dragons was their control of water, either in rivers, seas, lakes and wells, or as rain falling from the clouds. When angry they created storms, thunder and lightning but they could also bring about droughts by gathering up all the waters of a region into baskets. Because water was an essential life-giving element, the dragon was a symbol of fertility.

THE CHIMERA: A FEARSOME MIX

Not only dragons breathed fire. Flaming breath was also the weapon of the Chimera, a female monster with a lion's head, a goat's body and a serpent's tail.

The Chimera is described by Homer in his *Iliad*, where he tells how the hero Bellerophon kills the creature, 'an invincible inhuman monster, but divine in origin. She breathed deadly rage in searing fire.'

According to Hesiod, who talks of the Chimera in his

Theogony written in the 8th century BC, her parents were Echidna, goddess of illness and disease, and Typhon, god of winter storms, whose union also gave issue to other monsters, including the Hydra and Cerberus (see page 58). Hesiod describes a swift-footed creature with three heads, one from each component creature, and portrays the gallant Bellerophon riding astride the winged horse Pegasus (see page 236).

'Chimera' has become a generic name for weird creatures and fanciful notions, and also for animal and plant hybrids.

The three-headed form of the Chimera may have symbolized the cold of winter: her fire-breathing lion head being frost, her goat head winter storms, and her serpentine head sickness. The monster's name is derived from the Greek words *kheima*, cold, and *aera*, 'air'.

THE GHASTLY GRIFFIN

Also known as the griffon, gryphon or gryps, the griffin, like the dragon, is a mythological guardian of treasure. This winged creature has also been long employed as a protective emblem.

The griffin has the body of a lion and the head and wings of an eagle. Pliny, in his *Natural History*, writes of the struggle between the griffins and the Arimaspi, 'a people noted for having one eye in the middle of their forehead'. There was, he records, '… a continual battle between the Arimaspi and griffins in the vicinity of the latter's mines. The griffin,' he continues, 'is a type of wild beast with wings, as is commonly reported, which

The griffin is depicted on Minoan palaces on the island of Crete, where it is thought to act as a protective device. Much used in heraldry, since the 16th century it has been the badge of Grays Inn, one of the four Inns of Court in London that admit student lawyers wishing to become barristers.

digs gold out of tunnels. The griffins guard the gold and the Arimaspi try to seize it, each with remarkable greed.'

Griffins were renowned in Greek mythology for being the enemies of horses. They were also reputed to be responsible for pulling either the chariot of the sun across the sky each day or the chariot of the goddess Nemesis, the avenger of wrongdoing.

While female griffins were winged, the males were armed with spikes in place of wings. A variant of the griffin was the hyppogriff, which had a horse's body and an eagle's wings.

LUSTFUL DANCES OF THE SATYRS

Companions of the wine god Dionysus (the Roman Bacchus), and attendant at his revels, the satyrs were sylvan demigods that were part man and part animal.

The condition known to psychologists as satyr-iasis describes a man who has an uncontrollable desire to have sex with as many women as possible.

Inhabitants of woods and forests, the satyrs had goats' legs, pointed ears, small horns and human faces with upturned noses. Their tails were those of either horses or goats. Their arms were human. Decked with ivy or vine wreaths, they were sensual and pleasure loving, spending their time sleeping, playing musical instruments such as the flute, and performing lascivious dances with the nymphs.

The leader of the satyrs was Pan. The god of herds, he played a seven-reed shepherd's pipe, the 'Pan pipes' (see page 101). Travellers were taught to beware of waking Pan should they find him sleeping in a lonely place in the hills. If he was angered in this way he could send them fearful nightmares or simply terrify them with his loud voice.

SERPENT POWER

For good or ill (and mostly ill) snakes take on many different forms in stories from around the world. Some can fly, others live in water, and one is even large enough to embrace the earth.

A serpent that brought good fortune was the shahapet *or 'serpent ghost'. Kept indoors to bring luck to a household in winter this Indian beast was driven out into the fields in spring to ensure an abundant harvest.*

The ultimate symbol of evil, the Midgard Serpent or Jörmungandr, was the offspring of the trickster Loki and the sorceress Angur-boda, who also gave birth to Hel (the queen of the dead) and the Fenris Wolf (see page 239). Able to constrict and crush its victims, the venomous bite of the Midgard Serpent was deadly, even to the gods. The creature grew and grew and so, to combat its evil potential, Odin banished it to the depths of the sea. However it became so large that its body completely encircled the world.

It is said that at Ragnarök, the day when the gods will perish, the serpent will be killed by Thor, god of thunder and the serpent's enemy. According to the prophesy, the serpent will escape its underwater confinement. Thor will manage to kill it with his magic hammer, but will himself be murdered by the creature's deadly venom.

Apophis (or Apop), so the Egyptians believed, existed in total darkness in the underworld, bound in chains. Many-coiled and sometimes depicted with a human head, Apophis was the enemy of the sun god, Ra. Every night the serpent

The hornworm, whose existence was first reported in medieval times, was said to be a serpent with four horns. When it buried itself in sand only the horns could be seen; these were woven into a shining coronet, which the creature used to entice its prey. Apart from the fanciful crown and extra horns, this could be a description of a North American horned viper, an animal a traveller may well have encountered.

was thought to devour the sun as Ra rode through the abyss. Symbolic of the struggle between light and dark, Apophis lost the battle every night and the sun's victory was celebrated with each new dawn.

A MISCELLANY OF MYTHOLOGICAL SERPENTS

Amphiptère – *a winged serpent said to guard frankincense trees in Arabia.*

Meshekenabec – *a red-headed lake serpent with glistening scales and glowing eyes killed by the Great Hare of Algonquin legend.*

Lindorm – *a serpent-like Scandinavian beast with a leering mouth and cold, hypnotic eyes. Said to devour cattle.*

On Niont – *a huge horned serpent worshipped by the Huron Indians. Its horn could pierce mountains.*

Wyvern – *a winged serpent, a symbol of pestilence. A heraldic beast.*

Amphisbaena – *in Greek myth, a two-headed snake that terrorized the African desert: when one head was asleep the other was awake.*

HALF MAN, HALF HORSE

Of all the creatures with equine attributes, most famous are the centaurs of Greek mythology, some of whom formed part of the lascivious, abandoned retinue of Dionysus, the god of wine.

Having the legs and lower bodies of horses, and the torsos, arms and heads of men, the centaurs were diverse in their nature. While, as exemplified by Chiron, the virtuous teacher of Achilles, they were famed for their wisdom as teachers and healers, they could also be violent and lustful and, when drunk, were liable to attack and rape women.

Various legends surround the centaurs' origin. The most popular says that they were born as a result of the union

Were centaurs real? Pliny, the Roman naturalist, claimed to have seen a 'hippocentaur' embalmed in honey, which had been brought to Rome from Egypt.

between the treacherous Ixion and a cloud, which Zeus, as punishment for Ixion's seductive behaviour, had formed in the shape of the goddess Hera. Another maintains that they sprang to life when Zeus, displaying his passion for Aphrodite, spilt some of his sperm.

In a famous incident involving the centaurs, their half-brother Pirithous, the king of the fabulous Lapiths, invited them to his wedding feast, where they drank too much wine. One drunken centaur insulted the bride and a fearsome battle ensued in which many centaurs lost their lives. The remaining few were exiled from Thessaly.

Since their name means 'men who round up bulls', the centaurs are thought by scholars to be incarnations of the barbarous 'cowboys' of ancient Thessaly, in eastern Greece, who were renowned for their horsemanship as well as their lecherous behaviour.

One day, so legend relates, the Muses were singing and playing on Mount Helicon but were making so much noise that Poseidon sent Pegasus to quell their merriment. On arriving at the top of the mountain, Pegasus had only to paw the ground to quell the noise. From his footprint sprang the Hippocrene fountain, the source of poetic inspiration.

MAGICAL HORSES

Many gods and goddesses are credited with taking on the forms of horses, animals long revered for their strength and usefulness. And horses are believed, in many traditions, to help pull the sun across the sky.

Magical transformations are the stuff of mythology. To avoid the advances of Poseidon, the Greek sea god, the goddess Demeter transformed herself into a mare. But her efforts were in vain, for he turned himself into a stallion and as a result of their union they became parents to the magical winged black horse Arion. It was Arion who was later borrowed by Heracles in his labours.

Most divine of all the mythical horses was Pegasus, believed to have been created from the blood shed from the snake-headed Medusa (see page 210) after her head was severed by Perseus. Tamed by Bellerophon, with the help of a bridle given to him by the goddess Athene, Pegasus helped the hero defeat the Chimera (see page 231). But later, when Bellerophon tried to ride the horse up to the top of Mount Olympus – in order to reach heaven – Pegasus threw his rider off. Pegasus was then commandeered by Zeus to fetch and carry the thunder-bolts with which he attacked earth's mortal inhabitants.

> **Speed from fuel:**
> *The winged Pegasus is the logo of the Mobil corporation.*

THE SACRED BULL GIANT

Nowhere in the ancient world was the bull more sacred than on the island of Crete, where the legend of the Minotaur arose. With a man's body and a bull's head, this giant creature fed on human flesh.

The bull was the Cretan symbol of fertility – its strength and sexuality were believed to be concentrated in its horns. The Spanish bullfight almost certainly evolved from the bull-leaping rituals of ancient Crete.

In ancient Crete, goes the story, Pasiphaë, wife of King Minos of Crete, fell in love with a white bull, which appeared from the sea as a sign from Poseidon (ruler of the oceans) of Minos's sovereignty. To seduce the creature she hid herself inside a hollow wooden cow, covered with hide, which had been made for her by the cunning craftsman Daedalus. Together they wheeled it into the pasture where the bull was kept – and so the Minotaur was conceived and born.

To conceal his shame, Minos kept the Minotaur in a labyrinth at Knossos – which was also designed and made by Daedalus. Here the cannibalistic beast was regularly fed on the bodies of seven maidens and seven youths, all brought as tribute from Athens, which Minos had previously defeated in war, and left to wander the labyrinth's paths unaware of their fate. Present for the third of these 'sacrifice sessions' was Theseus, the son of King Aegeus of Athens, who planned to kill the creature with the help of Minos's daughter Ariadne. To prevent Theseus getting lost as he retraced his path through the maze, Ariadne gave him a skein of thread to mark his route, as well as the sword with which he performed his heroic feat.

> *The Minotaur was used as a symbol on the standard of one of the Roman legions.*

THE ONE-TUSKED ELEPHANT GOD

A pot-bellied man, short in stature, the elephant-headed, one-tusked Ganesha is the Hindu god of prosperity and good fortune. How his strange appearance came about is the subject of many stories.

Among Ganesha's notable features are a red body, a pot belly, a curved trunk, wide ears and four hands, one of which holds a rosary. His head is white. Why an elephant's head? One story tells how his mother, Parvati, showed off her son to the god Sani (the evil-eyed one), but when Sani glanced at the boy his head ignited and was burnt to ashes. On the advice of the god Brahma, Parvati replaced the head with whatever she could find – which turned out to be an elephant's head.

> *Although considered lazy and gluttonous, Ganesha is believed to be able to vanquish any obstacle he encounters. To accomplish this he rides on a mouse, who represents the power of the intellect to find its way through the most intricate problem and is always alert and active.*

The luck-bringing
power of the god
Ganesha is tradition-
ally invoked by Hindus
at the beginning of
journeys and important
tasks, and explains
why his image is often
included on the open-
ing pages of students'
notebooks.

And why one tusk? Ganesha was guardian of his parents' house, where he stood on duty outside the entrance to Shiva's room. When the hero Rama tried to enter the room, Ganesha tried to stop him, but Rama hurled an axe at Ganesha and severed one of his tusks. Or it may have been that, in his anger, Ganesha tore out one of his tusks and hurled it at the moon – which is how, in Hindu mythology, the waxing and waning of the moon is explained.

THE MIGHTY WOLF

Universally revered – and feared – the wolf takes on massive form and monstrous powers in ancient tales, especially those of Scandinavia. The Fenris Wolf even had the earth's destiny in its sights.

A huge monster in the form of a wolf, Fenris (or Fenrir) was not only strong but invulnerable. The gape of his jaws was so large that it reached between earth and heaven. Warned by an oracle that the Fenris Wolf, together with the Midgard Serpent, would be instrumental in the destruction of the earth, the gods decided that it must be kept under control. Since it quickly snapped every 'normal' rope used to tie it up, it was to be kept instead on a cord made by dwarfs and composed of six 'impossible' threads: the noise of a cat's footfall, the beards of women, the roots of a mountain, the sensibilities of a bear, the breath of fish, and the spittle of birds.

At Ragnarök, the twilight of the gods, the wolf will break free of his chains, join in battle against the gods and devour the great ruler Odin and with him the sun.

This confinement was not achieved without incident. Suspicious of what was to happen, the wolf insisted that if he was to be tied up, one of the gods would first have to put his hand in the animal's mouth. Only Tyr, the god of war, dared to do so – and lost a hand in the process – but the creature was successfully bound to a rock, called Gioll, with a sword clamped between his teeth to prevent him from biting.

WOLF FORMS

Many other mythological tales feature wolves:

- *A she-wolf tended and fostered Romulus and Remus, the twin founders of Rome.*
- *Hecate, the Greek goddess of the crossroads and the wilderness, was believed to take the form of a wolf.*
- *A wolf symbol was emblazoned on the shield of the huntress Artemis.*
- *In German legend, the Devil is said to have made the wolf's head from a stump of wood, its heart from stone and its breast from roots.*
- *Unbaptized children, says Finnish legend, wander the world in the shape of wolves.*

THE CHARMING SIRENS

The sweet singing of the Sirens was enough to lure sailors to disaster. These maidens – part human, part bird – were resisted by Odysseus and Jason, two great heroes of mythology.

When they heard the Sirens' beautiful melodies, sung from rocks off the Italian coast, sailors were doomed, it was said, because they were driven to steer their ships on to the rocks, or to jump into the sea and drown. Or they could be so besotted by the sound of the seductresses that they forgot everything – including food – and starved to death. Consequently the Sirens' island home was 'piled with boneheaps of men now rotted away'.

So how to resist the Sirens' lure? In the *Odyssey*, Homer tells how Odysseus was warned by Circe that any man listening to the Sirens, the 'enchanters of all mankind' had no prospect of coming home and 'delighting his wife and little children'. On her advice he ordered his men to stuff their ears with beeswax to prevent them from hearing the music. Odysseus, determined to hear the song, had himself tied to the ship's mast, so that he would be able to hear the Sirens' strains without steering or swimming to his death, though Circe warned, 'if you supplicate your men and implore them to set you free, then they must tie you fast with even more lashings'.

In the story of Jason and the Argonauts, the hero is saved from the Sirens' lure with the help of Orpheus, whose playing, reputed to be so sweet that it 'charmed the stones and trees to dance or to gather round him' outclassed that of the evil maidens.

SIREN MYTHS, SYMBOLS AND MEANINGS

- *In the Middle Ages, Sirens were commonly thought of as the souls of the dead with a malevolent envy of the living.*
- *Animals belonging to the order Sirenia, which include the manatee, are named for the Sirens.*
- *A siren is an instrument used to measure the frequency of vibrations in a musical note. It was named by the French physicist Charles Cagniard de la Tour.*
- *The two-toned siren call was used in World War II to warn of impending air raids, and to sound the all clear. The wartime leader Winston Churchill was renowned for favouring the all-in-one siren suit, originally designed to be pulled on quickly when taking cover in air raid shelters at night.*
- *A Siren is the logo of the Starbucks coffee corporation.*

THE IMMORTAL SIMURGH

Its name means 'like 30 birds' – a tribute to the size and power of the Simurgh, a bird said to be so old that it has not only seen the universe destroyed three times, but possesses all the knowledge of the ages.

The Simurgh's home is on the branches of the Tree of Knowledge. When it alights, so it is said, the sound of its wings is like thunder and the wind created by its wings blows the seeds of the Tree (the seeds of every plant that has ever existed) all over the world, so bringing all kinds of valuable plants to

Legend has it that the touch of the Simurgh's wing can heal even the most horrendous wounds.

the earth's human inhabitants. The Persian 11th-century epic *The Shahnama* tells of the Simurgh having 'energy from the falcon, power of flight from the Huma [phoenix], a long neck from the ostrich and a feathery collar from the ring dove …'

The 12th-century Persian author Farid al-Din Attar features the Simurgh in his allegory *The Parliament of Birds*, in which it represents ultimate spiritual unity. He describes it as:

… Truth's last flawless jewel, the light
In which you will be lost to mortal sight,
Dispersed to nothingness until once more
You find in Me the selves you were before.

In the poem, thousands of birds, under the leadership of the hoopoe, go on a pilgrimage in search of the Simurgh, during which they have to pass through the valleys of love, understanding, independence and detachment, unity, astonishment, poverty and, finally, nothingness. Lessons are learned from crossing each of the valleys and confronting the challenges they present. The story ends when 30 of the birds – the only survivors of the great expedition – realize that the Simurgh is actually their own transcendent totality.

BIRDS OF THE GODS

Herons, hummingbirds and woodpeckers are among the many birds that appear in myth and legend, often in human form.

The heron comes to life in the legend of Scylla, daughter of the Greek ruler Nisus, who, out of love for Minos, king of Crete, betrayed her father. As a result, Minos conquered Nisus's kingdom, but having done so, reneged on his engagement to Scylla in disgust at her treachery, and had her tied to the prow of a warship. However the gods of Olympus took pity on her and turned her into a heron. Her father Nisus, who had been killed in the battle, became a sea eagle and continually pursues his daughter, seeking revenge.

The Lydian carpenter Polytechnos was turned into a green woodpecker by an angry Zeus – after Polytechnos had been tricked by his wife into eating the flesh of his own child in revenge for raping her sister. In another myth it was said that the woodpecker ruled the earth until Zeus stole his sceptre.

Among native Americans the woodpecker is thought to protect children because of its habit of keeping its own young in such safety. Woodpeckers with red heads are said to have discovered fire by boring into wood.

On 21 October 1492, Christopher Columbus wrote in his journal of 'little birds ... so different from ours it is a marvel'. Huitzilopochitli, the 'hummingbird of the south' was, to the Aztecs, a god of sun and war. All warriors slain in battle, according to Aztec tradition, rise to the sky and orbit the sun for four years. They then become hummingbirds, feeding on flowers in paradise.

BEWARE THE BOGGART AND BUG-A-BOO

There are lots of good reasons for children to behave, not least the fear of weird animals (with weirder names) or little people with animal features that are coming to terrorize them.

The boggart, a type of Celtic hobgoblin, is a mischievous creature that often has fur, a tail or other animal accoutrements. Badly behaved children, especially in Yorkshire and Lancashire, are still threatened with being thrown into the 'boggart hole'. In its most evil form, which can haunt adults as well as children, the boggart – also called a shriker, barguest or trash – is a death omen that appears in the form of a white cow or horse, or sometimes as a black or white dog with massive paw pads, a shaggy coat and glaring eyes the size of saucers. Are boggarts real? In 1825, so one documented account relates, a Manchester tradesman was attacked by a huge headless dog, which put its feet on his shoulders and pushed him all the way home.

The bug-a-boo, also called the bodach or bugbear, will, it's said, kidnap naughty children. It comes down the chimney with no warning. Like the boggart, it probably gets its name from the Middle English word *bogge*, meaning 'terror'. When called bugbears they are thought, literally, to take on the shape of a bear and will actually eat their victims. They are sent, goes the old English proverb, 'to scare babes'.

THE LOTUS:
FLOWER OF CREATION

Life sprang, so Eastern tradition relates, from the lotus, the 'fairest flower'. Countless other stories, many linked to creation and fertility, are associated with the lotus – and with other plants of the same name.

The ancient Egyptians visualized that the world's supreme creator sprang from the blue lotus (*Nelumbo caerulea*), a type of water lily. Specifically, the sun god Horus (the falcon-headed deity) was believed to be reborn each morning from the water, having spent the previous night floating in the closed flower. As it opened its petals at dawn, the god emerged.

In ancient Indian religion the flower represents the womb of creation, from which all things are born. The goddess Padma, wife of the lotus-navelled god Vishnu, is also thought to have arisen from a lotus flower. She is often shown standing on a lotus being sprayed with water from elephants' trunks.

The myth expands. In the Hindu creation story Vishnu produces a lotus with 1000 golden petals on which the creator Brahma sits. From this flower, mountains arise and rivers and seas are made to flow.

In the Chinese Sacred Lake of Lotuses each soul is thought be represented by an individual lotus flower. After death, a soul is received by a lotus and exists within it, the subsequent health of the flower reflecting the sin or piety of the departed. The promise for the devout is that the lotus will open immediately after death, releasing the soul to the presence of the almighty Buddha.

IN THE FORM OF TREES

To fulfil his wish for everlasting gloom the unlucky youth Cyparissus was, according to legend, turned into a cypress tree. Other trees are also believed to be the living embodiments of people from the past.

Beloved of the god Apollo, the beautiful Cyparissus son of Telephus was given by him a sacred deer as a love token. The creature became the boy's constant companion, until a tragic accident occurred. One day, while the deer lay sleeping in a shady place amongst undergrowth, Cyparissus threw his javelin, which by unlucky accident hit and killed the deer. Grief-stricken, Cyparissus asked the gods that he be doomed to a future of eternal misery. So he was changed into a cypress tree, which, because it exudes droplets of sap from its trunk, has become a symbol of sorrow.

When their brother Phaeton died, the Heliades, the daughters of the sun god Helios, were so grief stricken that, out of compassion for their plight, the gods turned them into motionless, 'amber-oozing' trees beside the River Po. Historians are ambiguous about exactly which trees these are, but opinion favours the black poplar over the alder.

In another tree story linked with Apollo, the nymph Daphne, fleeing from his attentions, prayed to the gods for assistance. They answered her supplications by turning her into a laurel (bay). Finding that he was no longer touching soft flesh but bark, Apollo crowned his head with the leaves and the tree became sacred to him.

MORE TREE TALES

- *Overcome with shame at giving birth to a centaur, the Greek goddess Philyra turned herself into a linden tree.*
- *Having been bewitched by Aphrodite, and then seduced her own father, Myrrha was converted by shame into a myrrh tree. Her son Adonis emerged from the tree.*
- *As a reward for unwittingly offering hospitality to Zeus the aged couple Philemon and Baucis were turned, after their death, into an oak and a linden growing next to each other so that they would never be parted.*
- *The beautiful nymph Pitys was loved by both Pan and Boreas, the north wind. When she chose Pan, Boreas blew her over a cliff. Gaia, the earth goddess, took pity on her and turned her into a pine tree. When the north wind blows through the tree you can, it's said, still hear her weeping.*

IN FLORAL FORM

Among the world's most beautiful flowers are some long thought to be mortals in disguise. The stories live on in the symbolism of these favourite blooms.

Provided he never saw his own image – it was prophesied by Tiresias the seer – the beautiful boy Narcissus would live a long and happy life. When out hunting one day (having, incidentally, spurned the love of the nymph Echo) he stopped to quench his thirst in a stream. There he saw and fell in love with his own reflection. So spellbound that he was unable to move, he pined to death and was changed by the gods into his eponymous flower 'with tufts of white about the button crowned'.

Psychologists use the term 'narcissism' to describe excessive self-admiration.

The hyacinth sprang, it is said, from the blood of Apollo in his remorse for the death of the boy of the same name. Hyacinth fell victim to the jealous rage of Zephyrus (god of the west wind) who, when Hyacinth was playing quoits with Apollo, blew so powerfully on Apollo's iron plaything that it struck Hyacinth and killed him.

The flower of the myth related here may not have been the hyacinth we know today but the red Martagon lily. This is bound up with the belief that Hyacinth's last cry was 'Ai, ai,' words that can be seen as marks on the flower's petals.

Blood shed in death led to the creation of the pheasant's eye or Adonis flower. The boy Adonis (born from a myrrh tree) was loved by Aphrodite. When Adonis was killed by a wild boar the goddess was so sorrowful that she made a red flower spring from his blood. The gods agreed to let Adonis spend half the year on earth and half in the underworld, a story that symbolizes the annual dying of vegetation in autumn and its return in spring.

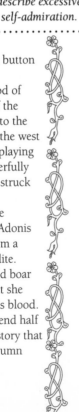

INDEX